ON AN(ARCHY) & SCHIZOANALYSIS

ON AN(ARCHY)
& SCHIZOANALYSIS

ROLANDO PEREZ

AUTONOMEDIA

Special thanks to Sue Ann Harkey and Rolando Perez.
Illustrations from *Optical and Geometrical Allover Patterns*,
by Jean Larcher, courtesy Dover Publications, Inc.

Autonomedia
55 South 11th Street
POB 568 Williamsburgh Station
Brooklyn, New York
11211-0568 USA

718 387-6471

Printed in the United States of America

CONTENTS

ON AN(ARCHY)
& SCHIZOANALYSIS

FIRST
PLATEAU

"[O]ur sentence does not sound severe. Whatever commandment the prisoner has disobeyed is written upon his body by the Harrow. This prisoner, for instance"—the officer indicated the man—"will have written upon his body: HONOR THY SUPERIORS!"
> Kafka
> *The Penal Colony*

The body is the body, /it is alone/and has no need of organs, /the body is never an organism/organisms are the enemies of bodies, /everything one does transpires by itself without the aid of any organ, /every organ is a parasite, /it overlaps with a parasitic function into existence which should not be there...It is/I/who/will be/remade/by myself/entirely/...by myself/who am a body/and have no regions within me.
> Antonin Artaud

1

NIETZSCHE, AN(ARCHY) AND ANTI-PSYCHIATRY*

Perhaps it seems odd that one should write an essay associating Nietzsche with anarchy. However, the an(archy) which I propose to attribute to Nietzsche is not the political anarchy which he wrote against.

Moreover it must also seem strange to have Nietzsche associated with a movement in psychology that has come so many years after his death and which remains even today a fringe "movement." But I think there are certain connections

---

*Firstly, I have decided to to use the word "anti-psychiatry" as a generic term to include both the type of analysis done by people like Laing and Cooper and the "schizoanalysis" done by Deleuze and Guattari. And secondly, I have spelled the word *an(archy)* to differentiate it from traditional political anarchy.

to be made here between these modern concepts and Nietzsche. And so works by Laing, Cooper, and Deleuze and Guattari will be used in order to establish this connection.

With regard to an(archy), my intention herein is to: (1) approach the topic via deconstruction, or more specifically via Derrida, and (2) via Deleuze's and Guattari's "schizoanalysis" in order to demonstrate what it is that I mean by an(archy) and how this concept of an(archy) is latently found in Nietzsche.

However, before we turn to the issue of an(archy), we must first turn to the more primordial issue of Nietzsche's concept of "forgetfulness" and the "innocence of becoming," for without these concepts the an(archy) proposed by Nietzsche is not possible at all.

1

Right after Zarathustra's prologue the first section we come to is the section "On the Three Metamorphoses." Here Nietzsche describes to us a certain change that must take place if we are to have a new beginning. He writes:

> Of the three metamorphoses of the spirit I tell you: how the spirit becomes a camel, and the camel a lion; and the lion, finally, a child.[1]

As such, a change must take place, from that which is physically big to that which is physically small and from that which is fully grown to that which is about to grow. But there is also a sense in which the spirit like the camel has had too much to bear — that the weight has become such that "the straw has finally broken the camel's back." At this point, then, the lion becomes the spirit. That is, the spirit that opposes the slowly rotting carcass of the camel in the desert sun. And while the lion is the "nay saying" spirit and the spirit of freedom (the spirit which has renounced *duty*), he is too old to be the spirit of the beginning and the spirit of forgetfulness.

"To create new values — " says Nietzsche,

> that even the lion cannot do; but the creation of freedom for oneself, for new creation, that is within the power of the lion. The creation of freedom for oneself and a sacred "No" even to duty — for that, my brother, the lion is needed.[2]

Thus it is the liberating roar of the lion which announces the death of reactive morality, or what is usually referred to as "the morality of habit." And the new man/woman on the horizon is the *over(wo)man* (the active as opposed to the reactive type) — or to put it another way the "spirit of the child." But why a child?

> The child is innocence and forgetting, a new beginning, a game, a *self-propelled* wheel, a first movement, a sacred "Yes."[3] (my italics).

And since part of a child's nature is to play,

> play represents an activity that does not aim at any practical utilitarian needs and ends, being unconcerned with good and evil, truth and falsity.[4]

In summary, then, the child, this "self-propelled wheel" moves forward, forever forward, disseminating the old concepts of binary opposites. And at last, at last a morality *"jenseits von gut und böse"*!

2

Here, then, is where Nietzsche's an(archy) comes in. For just as Derrida's *differance* disseminates the hier(archical) binary opposites, so does Nietzsche's *"jenseits."* Hence the concept of *"jenseits"* or "beyond" is not to be interpreted in a Hegelian manner, but more appropriately in the Derridean sense of *differance,* i.e., in a disseminating manner. As Nietzsche writes:

> Habit of seeing opposites. — The general imprecise way of observing sees everywhere in nature opposites (as e.g., "warm and cold") where there are, not opposites but *differences* or degrees...[5] (my italics).

It is living in the (/) of *differance,* that is, beyond... that makes life dangerous, and yet it is precisely this that Nietzsche challenges us to undertake.

> The dangerous and uncanny point has been reached where the greater, more manifold, more comprehensive life transcends and *lives beyond* the old morality... [6] (Nietzsche's italics).

One must live dangerously, says Nietzsche. One must be willing to walk the rope over the abyss (*Abgrund*) and in so doing deny the spirit of the reactive forces that pull us down. And for this one must have courage. Why? Simply because to live *beyond*, in the (/), is to live no-where: to live as a human being independent of the morality of exclusive binary oppositions, foundations, and institutions. However, this is not to say that Nietzsche's project involved the wholesale dissolution of moral hier(archical) oppositions.

What Nietzsche wanted above all was (1) to go beyond moral hier(archical) oppositions so as to disseminate them in order to make them free flowing rather than fixed; and (2) to go beyond the inscription of institutional hier(archical) structures in order to undermine the repressive coding of institutions. In addition to this, the affirmation of rank one finds in Nietzsche's works serves as the best example that Nietzsche's an(archy) was the first non-political an(archy) and, of course, the first truly structureless an(archy) in the history of philosophy. The famous master-slave morality delineated by Nietzsche makes it very difficult for anyone to view an(archy) as either an ideology of the Right or of the Left — especially since it is the active, self-governing (and not necessarily "political") individual whom he values.

> In Nietzsche, the word *hierarchy* has two senses. It signifies firstly, the difference between active and reactive forces, the superiority of active to reactive forces, and the complex organisation which results — where the weak have conquered, where the strong are contaminated, where the slave who has not appeared prevails over the master who has stopped being one: the reign of *law* and virtue. If we compare the

two senses we see that the second is like the
reverse of the first. We make the Church, morality and the State the masters and keepers of
all hierarchy[7] (my italics).

And it is precisely this second sense of hier(archy)
that Nietzsche is against. For this is the hier(archy) of institutions and eco-political frameworks set up by those who cannot lead or obey themselves: of the weak and the slaves and
of those who need an outside hier(archical) authority in order to act.

For Nietzsche, then, slave morality is the morality of
paranoiac machines who inscribe all their fears onto the body
without organs and turn the body w/o organs into a "body
of laws": in the name of "alliance" and community self-preservation.

The law, the thoroughly realistic *formalization*
of certain conditions for the self-preservation
of a community, forbids certain actions directed
against the community: it does not forbid the
disposition that produces these actions—for it
needs these for other ends, namely against the
enemies of the community[8] (N's italics).

This inscription or coding onto the social field is the
product of the reactive fear to "live dangerously," to live in
the (/) of differance, which calls for a constant questioning
of all values: ending if one may put it as such in a certain
"ethical an(archy)." That is to say, in a structureless, non-
coded, non-inscribed morality, or perhaps more appropriately "immorality."

On the other hand we have the community which sets

up the despotic State machinery in order to "breed man." Or as Nietzsche puts it:

> Morality is a menagerie. Its presupposition is that iron bars can be more profitable than freedom , even for prisoners; its other presupposition is that there exist animal trainers who are not afraid of terrible means — who know how to handle red hot iron. This frightful species which takes up the fight against the wild animal is called the "priest"...[9]

and one may very well add the "despot" to this.

> All the stupidity and the arbitrariness of the laws, all the pain of the institutions, the whole perverse apparatus of repression and education, the red-hot irons, and the atrocious procedures have only this meaning: to breed man, to mark him in his flesh, to render him capable of alliance...[10]

And what better example do we have of this than Hitler? For after all one does not only brand or inscribe (e.g., the numbers on the arm) in order to create alliance but also and perhaps more importantly to differentiate those inside the community from those outside. The outsider is always a threat, for it is he or she — the misfit — who usually questions the *order* of things. And as we all know everything must always be "nice, neat, and orderly" for a paranoiac machine, and especially of course if that paranoiac machine happens to be military, political or economic. In Albert Camus' *Caligula*, after Caligula has *ordered* the poets to read their poems he turns to Cherea and whispers: "you see, organization's needed for everything, even art."[11] That's why the political "will to order" is usually a will to violence and oppression.

And yet a word of warning is needed: an(archy), the dissemination of external hier(archical) structures, does not imply an "anything-goes ideology," a violent thunderbolt that will create more violence than the institutions themselves, after all this is what an(archy) as a project sets out to prevent, i.e., the violent thunderbolt of State, Church, mental institutions, etc.

> Where the state *ends* — look there, my brothers! Do you see it, the rainbow and the bridges of the overman?[12] (N's italics).

For the overman or over(wo)man is she who no longers needs the State, or any other institution, for that matter. She is is her own creator of values and as such the first true an(archist). In short, she rejects all external orders. She is her own master.[13] She is the first renouncer of the traditional morality which codes, inscribes, and fixes the "oppositions" of the world in an exclusive hier(archical) framework so as to make life safe when in fact "chaos is needed to offset the tendency to stagnation."[14] And yet the over(wo)man is not merely a type but more importantly a process, a flow, a line of flight, a rhizome (Deleuze/Guatarri).

However, one must beware of the danger that lies herein, for there is always the possibility that the unimpeded ("over-(wo)man") process, the unrestricted flow, the body without organs, may go in any direction, including the opposite direction desired. Which is why the an(archical) release of the over-coded, overinscribed flows of desire must come about gradually rather than all at once. The life that is lived in the

(/) of *differance*, in the "beyond," is a highly dangerous life whose positivity is dependent upon the way that one comes to it.

The violence unleashed by youth gangs and other *micro-fascist* groups (Guattari) around the world today is the result of non-structured, non-coded, non-inscribed flows of desire, but this is not what either Nietzsche, Deleuze, Guattari or Laing have in mind. As Deleuze and Guattari have pointed out in *On the Line:*

> There is desire as soon as there is... a body without organs. But there are bodies without organs that are empty, hardened envelopes because their organic components have been eliminated too quickly and forcefully, as in an "overdose." There are cancerous or fascist bodies without organs, in black holes or in machines of abolition.[15]

And in *The Death of the Family,* Cooper also warns against a too-sudden elimination of the coding or inscribing hier(archical) (familial) frameworks. The autonomy which results from the process Cooper calls "Ekonia," "Paranoia," and "Anoia" can lead to disastrous effects if it is not achieved gradually. He writes:

> There is, of course, much room for confusion of location between these stages, one of the most disastrous being the attempt to move from ekonia and paranoia to anoia without the requisite of self-containing autonomy[16]

or what Nietzsche called "self-sovereignty."

Thus, in the end a new psychology is needed — a psychology that will help us to undertake the task of gradually releasing our over-coded flows of desire without putting us back in a mental institution. In sum, such psychology is anti-psychiatry, and what Deleuze and Guattari call "schizo-analysis."

3

Anti-psychiatry is the first an(archistic) psychology, and as such the first to promote the breakdown of hier(archical) institutional frameworks and the "family" in particular. In that vein Deleuze and Guattari's "schizoanalysis" is a critique and a going beyond of the Freudian Oedipal structure which determines the life of the individual by making him or her dependent on the *internalized* "mommy, daddy, and me" structure. As the above authors see it: the Oedipal structure is one of the major causes of schizophrenia.

Yet what is being opposed is not the child-parent relationship *per se* but the Oedipalization of such a relationship.

> It is not a question of denying the vital importance of parents or the love attachment of children to their mothers and fathers. It is a question of knowing what the place and the function of parents are within desiring-production, rather than doing the opposite and forcing the

entire interplay of desiring machines* to fit within (*rabattre tout le jeu des machines desirantes dans*) the restricted code of Oedipus.[17]

This structuralization and control of desire is clearly what Nietzsche is against, for we might recall that the child is important for Nietzsche precisely because she is... always free, non-coded, and non-inscribed. The child is a body without organs and insofar as she has parents, her parents are not those who bring her up, who inscribe upon her body the inscription inscribed upon them by their parents (and their parents' parents, and so on).** The true child is she who surpasses her parents, she who goes beyond them to such an extent that eventually she leaves them behind as she walks into the desert as the first true nomad: "the self-propelled wheel" who does not look back. In *Zarathustra* Nietzsche writes:

> You shall create a *higher body* [a body w/o organs perhaps?], a first movement, a self-propelled wheel—you shall create the creator. Marriage thus I name the will of two to create the one that is more than whose who created it.

---

* Like a streetcar named "Desire," whose direction is controlled by the lines which run beneath it, the restrictiveness of the Oedipal structure leads to the control of desiring-machines and their uncoded flows of desire. What we have in the end, then, is simply another schizoprehenic Blanche DuBois and another despotic Stanley Kowalski.

** This complex familial overcoding of values is what R.D. Laing calls the "knots" which can eventually lead to schizophrenia.

> Reverence for each other, as for those willing
> with such a will is what I name marriage[18] (my
> italics).

And the product of such a marriage is a child who is not
afraid to smash all our repressive machines.[19]

"The lights jigging like electric needles. The atoms going
crazy with light and heat. A conflagration going on behind
the glass and nothing burns away," writes Miller.

> Men breaking their backs, men bursting their
> brains to invent a machine which a child will
> manipulate. If I could only find the hypotheti-
> cal child who's to run this machine I'd put a
> hammer in its hands and say: Smash it! Smash
> it![20]

And yes, she'll smash it alright. This child is free... free of
guilt! (Not because she does exactly what she has been
brought up to do, but rather because she has not been subjected to the kind of bodily and psychological overcoding
that most children are subjected to).

No one is born with a sense of guilt. Guilt is the result
of familial inscription or overcoding. How close one remains
to mommy and daddy or how far one strays from them determines the degree of someone's sense of guilt.* "If there is
perfect coincidence between the values projected or alloted
to a range, everything is in its proper time and place," writes
Laing.

---

* The family turns the child's body (or body without organs) into a
  "docile body" (Foucault) and a "soft machine" (Burroughs).

There is no infringement of the rules on this set
of issues, and no need for guilt or anxiety on
these grounds... One is good oneself if one has
good thoughts about what one is supposed to
think good about, and bad thoughts about what
one is supposed to think bad about.[21]

But what if there is no "perfect coincidence" between the
values of the child and the values of the family? How can the
child break away then without feeling "guilty"? After all, the
family overcodes, overinscribes and overmaps its values on
the child; and all the rules it inscribes on him or her are
protected by meta-rules, meta-meta-rules and so on. Which,
of course, makes the "re-evaluation" and the going beyond
of (traditional) family values if not impossible, extremely difficult.

Rules govern all aspects of experience, *what* we
are to experience, and what *not* to experience,
the operations we must and must not carry out,
in order to arrive at a permitted picture of ourselves and others in the world. But a special
situation exists if there is a rule against examin-
ing or questioning values: and beyond that, if
there are rules against even being aware that
such rules exist, including this last rule (Laing's
italics).[22]

This is why the breaking of rules, the going beyond of
traditional (family) morality is so very difficult. One must
somehow be able to see through the rules and all the restric-
tions behind them. And then to make matters even more
difficult, one must be willing take a chance with one's so-

called "sanity" in order to break the rules. No wonder then most traditional forms of anarchy have resorted to communal arrangements in order to solve this problem.

"How do I disconnect without losing my head?" "How do I disconnect without becoming a criminal?" It is extremely difficult to erase the emotional (albeit negative) attachments inscribed by the family. And it is this feeling (the terrible feeling of guilt) which gives rise to communal arrangements.

Unfortunately, these communal arrangements usually don't work. The moment they institute a leader — and most of them do — they also institute a hier(archical) structure not too different from that of most families.

Cooper's experiment with anti-psychiatric communes as replacements for established psychiatric institutions failed precisely because it set up a new institution in place of the old one. Insofar as Cooper was the organizer of the commune he was, whether he liked it or not, a "false leader," to use his own terminology. He was *the* psychiatrist and remained so whether he called himself a "member," a "comrade" or an "equal." The problem of familialism is exclusively one of interiority. It is possible that one may live under the same roof with one's family and not be fucked up by it; on the other hand there are people who live in the South Pole for whom the (internal) "family" is always there regulating and overcoding their flows of desire. That's why

> even with the progressive or revolutionary sectors of institutional analysis on the one hand, and anti-psychiatry on the other, the danger of this familialism is ever present, conforming to the double impasse of an extended Oedipus, just as much in the diagnostic of pathogenic

families in themselves, as in the constitution of therapeutic quasi-families [or communes].[23]

4

In the final analysis, the aim of anti-psychiatry, or more specifically schizoanalysis, is to release the hier(achical) and internal familial structures inscribed upon the body without organs. "In some families," says Laing,

> parents cannot allow children to break the "family" down within themselves, if that is what they want, because this is felt as the breakup of the family, and then where will it end?[24]

To which several answers come to mind, as for example: action, desire, innocence, creativity, an(archy) and freedom! But unfortunately for the child "the 'family' may be an internal structure more important than the 'breast,' 'penis,' or 'father'."[25] These internal structures are inscribed by the family on the child's psyche in order to diminish the child's own potential for self-directed action or what Nietzsche called the "innocence of becoming."

> As soon as we imagine someone responsible for our being thus and thus... and therefore attribute to him the intention that we should exist and be happy or wretched, we corrupt for ourselves the *innocence of becoming.*[26]

And as soon as we incribe upon the child's body without organs the hier(archical) familial structure, then he or she becomes a reactive rather than a active individual, a rigid line rather than a line of flight; and his or her potentiality for selfmastery and autonomy is denied. In conclusion: what we have here is a segmented and rigid line which overcodes and overinscribes the rules and metarules by which the individual is to progress. "As individuals and groups," writes Deleuze,

> we are made of lines, lines that are very diverse in nature. The first type of line (there are many of this type) that form us is segmentary, or rigidly segmented: family/profession; work/ vacation; family/ then school/ then army/ then factory/and then retirement. Each time from one segment to another, we are told, "Now you are no longer a child"; then at school "Now you are no longer at home"; then in the army, "This isn't school any more"... In short, all kinds of well-defined segments, going in every direction, which carve us up in every sense, these bundles of segmented lines.[27]

Thus what an(archy) and schizoanalysis aim at is the replacement of poor defenseless, guilt-ridden puppets in internal straight-jackets, with free, non-Oedipalized, uncoded individuals.

SECOND
PLATEAU

Language has always been the companion of empire.
Antonio de Nebrija

The letter kills the spirit... life in general is mobility itself.
Henri Bergson
Creative Evolution

To suggest that the signifier is everywhere (and that consequently interpretation and transference are effective everywhere) is to miss the fact that each of these encoding components (whether semiotic or not) can gain power over the situation and objects confronting us. On the contrary, I believe that one should not be dogmatic about which mode of access has priority. Such priority can emerge only from analysing each particular situation...Experts in linguistics and semiotics have gradually come to consider that icons, or diagrams, or any other preverbal means of expression (gestural, etc.) are dependent upon the signifying language and are only imperfect means of communication. I believe that this is an intellectualist assumption that becomes extremely shaky when applied to children, the mad, the primitive or any of those who express themselves in a semiotic register that I would classify as a symbolic semiology.
Félix Guattari
Molecular Revolution

2

AU REVOIR M. LE TEXTE, OR, THE BODY AND AN(ARCHY)

It is no exaggeration to say that we have gone much too far with our emphasis on the Text, or what amounts to the same, with the written Text. Along with this overdose, most of it which has come from France, we have forgotten the body, the theater, the gesture, the breath (*souffle*) and the flesh. Perhaps, then, it is time that we start giving the same importance to the body that we have given to the Text.

So let us attempt to examine the overlooked relation between the written text and the body as a symbolic or a-signifying expression.* Let us take Roland Barthes as the

---

* We must keep in mind that by the word *expression* we mean something completely different than what Saussure means by it or what Barthes or Eco means by it. There is no content or signified (Saussure), no signification (Barthes), no sender and receiver (Eco), and in short no David

examplar of those who have emphasized the former (i.e., the written Text) and Artaud as an examplar of the rare individual who emphasizes the body as expression, as breath, as gesture. And in the process let us also make an attempt to demonstrate the points on which they agree, as for example their rejection of the Author-God position, their rejection of repetition, and their concern with bringing either the Reader (Barthes) or the Spectator (Artaud) closer to the written Text or the theater.

Let's view this problematic, then, in light of a double-articulation,[1] namely in a non-exclusive and relative manner. It is in this respect that we say "au revoir M. le Texte." Which is not to say that one is dogmatically dismissing the Text once and for all, but merely that a non-exclusive shift in emphasis is needed if we are to recover our relation to our bodies.

1

We should not take it as a coincidence that with the death of God there should also have come the death of the Author: the Creator of Masterpieces. Artaud was one of the first to

---

Sarnoff here. And this type of expression does indeed exist. For instance, in reference to the Guayaki Indians that Pierre Clastres writes about in *Chronique de Indiens Guayaki*, Guattari (*Molecular Revolution*) notes that "The strata of expression are not regulated by a signifying control that condemns every content to a rigorous formalization, a residual or marginal representation; here, this polyvocal concept of the Jaguar becomes the object of a fluid, uncertain, wavering denotation, a denotation unsure of itself, in some cases even with no basis at all, a pure denotation of denotation." (p 93).

have declared the Author dead. And in the last fifteen to twenty years he has been followed by such critics as Ricoeur, Derrida, and Roland Barthes. As Derrida has pointed out in his essay "The Theater of Cruelty," the

> stage is theological for as long as its structure following the entirety of tradition, comports the following elements: an author-creator who, absent and from afar, is armed with a text and keeps watch over, assembles, regulates the time or meaning of representation, letting this latter represent him as concerns what is called the content of his thoughts, his intentions, his ideas.[2]

Artaud responded to this calling for the death of the Author-Creator* by replacing the Author with the theater and the "director."

> In this theater all creation comes from the stage, finds its expression and its origin alike in a secret psychic impulse which is Speech before Words.[3]

The written word becomes secondary and the Author is displaced by the voice which shouts and speaks. Artaud continues:

> It is a theater which eliminates the author in favor of what we would call, in our Occidental

---

* Forget the Father, forget Oedipus, forget even the Name-of-the-Father. As Brando says in "Last Tango in Paris," "there will be no names here," no family history, and thus no referentiality.

theatrical jargon, the director, but the director
who has become a kind of manager of magic, a
master of sacred ceremonies. And the material
on which he works, the themes he brings to
throbbing life are derived not from him but from
the gods.[4]

The director, therefore, is a shaman, not a Creator or hierar-
chical figure — but merely the mediator of magic. Roland
Barthes, on the other hand, considered the Author dead but
the written Text very much alive. In fact, for Barthes the
Author dies not only in the name of the Reader but more
importantly in the name of the Text.

As Barthes pointed out in "The Death of the Author":

The removal of the Author (...) is not merely an
historical fact or an act of writing; it utterly
transforms the modern text (or — which is the
same thing — the text as henceforth made and
read in such a way that at all levels the author
is absent).[5]

And later in the same essay he writes:

We know now that the text is not a line of words
releasing a single theological meaning (the
"message" of the Author-God) but a multidi-
mensional space in which a variety of writings,
none of them original, blend and clash. The text
is a tissue of quotations drawn from innumer-
able centres of culture.[6]

In effect, the text is a non-originary plane of multiplicities, a field of traces left "behind" by a multiplicity of writers, none of them belonging to any one particular tribe. The problem with Barthes is that for him the world becomes Text and the Text — or Signifier/Signified relation — is exalted to the place formerly occupied by the Author. The Text is now made God.

Conversely, for Artaud, the death of the Author takes place right along with the death of the written Text: the Signifier, the Word. For Artaud words cannot express that which is most profound. It is only the theater of cruelty — the theater of life — that can give expression to the human breath and to the flesh. As Derrida has said: Artaud's protest is directed "against the dead letter which absents itself far from breath (*souffle*) and flesh."[7]

> The classical Western stage defines a theater of the organ, a theater of words, thus a theater of interpretation, energistration, and translation, a theater of deviation from the groundwork of a pre-established text, a table written by a God-Author who is the sole wielder of the primal word.[8]

This is precisely what Artaud was against. Unlike Barthes and others Artaud believed that both the Author and the written Text had to be subordinated to the theater of the flesh. In the second manifesto of "The Theater of Cruelty" he wrote: "We shall renounce the theatrical superstition of the text and the dictatorship of the writer."[9] Artaud did not subordinate the Author without also subordinating the Text.

Moreover, while Roland Barthes subordinated the Author to the Reader of the Text, Artaud subordinated the Author to the spectator of the play. "The reader," says Barthes,

> is the place on which all the quotations that
> make up a writing are inscribed without any of
> them being lost; a text's unity lies not in its
> origin but in its destination.[10]

The reader is given the place of the decipherer who gives meaning to the text by his or her own interaction with the text. Barthes' proposal to diminish the distance between the Reader and the Text is analogous to Artaud's proposal to bring the specatator closer to the stage.

> We abolish the stage and the auditorium and
> replace them by a single site, without partition
> or barrier of any kind, which will become the
> theater of the action. A direct communication
> will be re-established between the spectator and
> the spectacle, between the actor and the specta-
> tor, from the fact that the spectator, placed in
> the middle of the action, is engulfed and physi-
> cally affected by it.[11]

The distance between the spectator and the actor is obliterated in much the same way that Barthes obliterates the distance between the Author and the Reader: by placing the Reader at the place of the Text. But, while Barthes is erecting temples to his Text Artaud is burning them down: to replace the Great Occidental temples of the Text with the theater of the flesh, the theater of passion and desiring-pro-duction, where expression is not linguistic but hieroglyphic and *a-signifying* in nature. At last, then, we have the *flows* of the body replace the flows of words. And linguistic expression is replaced by the emotive *a-signification* of "affective athleticism." After all, "it has not been definitely proved that the language of words is the best possible language."[12] And gestures, dances, and shouts become the superseding alternative to the kind of semiotic (signifying) reading performed by people like Eco and Todorov.

The gesture is always spontaneous, non-coded and non-inscribed; and it disappears like a musical note the moment it is performed. But most importantly, unlike the despotic and imperialistic Signifier it does not refer back to anything; it is not circular but linear. Yes, one may perhaps go so far as to say that the body is a "text" for Artaud, but it is certainly not a linguistic text. Artaud himself called for the hieroglyphic signs of the East which are always "metaphysical" rather than psychological and linguistic in nature.

2

Again, Artaud turned to the East in order to find there what he found lacking in Western culture. That is to say, in order to find his theater of "carnal and metaphysical signs." Barthes, on the other hand, turned to the East in search of his "Cabinet of Signs," and found, in Japan his Great Empire of Signs.

> Now it happens that in this country [Japan] the empire of the signifier is so immense, so in excess of speech, that the exchange of signs remains a fascinating richness, mobility, and subtlety, despite the opacity of the language, sometimes even as a consequence of that opacity.[13]

Artaud, however, turned to the Orient to recover the human relation to the flesh, the non-coded flows of desire, and the expressive innocence of the gesture. "The Balinese theater," he wrote, "has revealed to us a physical and non-verbal idea of the theater..."[14] And later: "For the Occidental theater the Word is everything, and there is no possibility of expression without it," therefore even "if we restrict theater to what happens between cues, we have still not managed to separate it from the idea of a *performed text*."[15]

We have erected so many temples to the Signifier that the Signifier has even illicitly entered the unconscious via a certain port in France called Lacan. The Western world has become a world of linguistic signs in which reality has come to equal the famous (or perhaps infamous) Signifier–Signified relation.

The perfect example of this obsession with words is found in Umberto Eco's *A Theory of Semiotics* where he goes on to propose in an interesting way a "possible world" problem in which snow would be made of peanut butter. "Every English speaker," says he,

> can speak about snow and understand sentences concerning snow because he possesses a cultural competence assigning to the content unit 'snow' certain properties which do not include that of being made with peanut butter. It is possible that in a possible world or in our future world, because of the increasing water pollution, snow cold be exposed to such an ecological tragedy. But even though it happened, the fact would still be semiotically ridiculous.[16]

And then Eco goes on to say that the great problem facing us under such circumstances would be that of changing our sign-system in order to accomodate the new phenomenon. This, I think, is exemplary of the Western obsession with words which has reached its zenith with structuralism and poststructuralist literary criticism — no one excluded.

In the West we have even used the uninscribed body (or as Deleuze and Guattari call it "the body without organs") as a recording surface. "Merely so many nails piercing the flesh, so many forms of torture."[17] Perhaps a reminder of Kafka's "In The Penal Colony" is in order. Here the Harrow inscribes the body with piercing needles and the words "HONOR THY SUPERIORS" are inscribed upon the body to create a memory, a text, a masterpiece, to torture, to cause a slow and painful death. And yet one finds someone like Barthes so proud of this affair! "The theatrical face," he says, "is not painted (made-up), it is written."[18] And further down: "it is the act of writing which subjugates the pictorial gesture so that to paint is never anything but to inscribe."[19] Artaud's enterprise was, of course, different: he was concerned with the gestural *expressiveness* of the body, as opposed to the writing *on* the body that the hyperliterate Barthes so much admired.

No longer should we speak solely of the Great Text, but we should begin to speak as we once did of the hieroglyphics of gestures... of the body... and of the flesh. No longer must we apply "piercing needles" to the body. The expression of cruelty will be a "metaphysical" and symbolic expression as opposed to a physical one. The rigor of the necessity of life will take place right before one's eyes without the need of a "Harrow" or pen. There will be no spurt of blood but flows which are not the result of a puncture. Gestures will take the place of words inscribed upon the *body without organs.* The gesture will replace the even and calculated speech of the West which no longer expresses anything alive. And unlike one of Beckett's characters we will not say "I shall remain silent" and continue to speak. Gestures will displace the emptiness of the spoken Signifier. Barthes' voyage to the Land of Signs where he finds the Signifier even in an eyelid is positionally replaced by Artaud's voyage to the flesh. But we must keep in mind, however, that this is only a temporary voyage. We are the enemies of colonialism. And we are not proposing an Empire of the Body.

No more masterpieces, no more masters (forget Hegel!), no more writing. "All writing is pigshit."[20] Why? Because our innermost feelings are untranslatable and linguistically inexpressible, "and people who leave the obscure and try to define whatever it is that goes on in their heads are pigs."[21] And

> those for whom certain words have a meaning, and certain manners of being; those who are so fussy; those for whom emotions are classifiable, and who quibble over some degree or other of their hilarious classifications; those who still believe in 'terms'; those who brandish whatever ideologies belong to the hierarchy of the times... those who follow paths, who drop names, who fill books with screaming headlines are the worst kind of pigs.[22]

Yet Artaud did not want to do way with the language of words altogether. What he wanted was to libertate our psyches and our bodies from the state of hyperliteracy which has made us schizophrenic indidviduals.

"The literate man when we meet him in the Greek world is a split man," says Marshall McLuhan, "a schizophrenic, as all men have been since the invention of the phonetic alphabet."[23] Thus, it is Barthes' split world, i.e., the world of the Text and world of the body, that Artaud finds culturally and existentially objectionable.

> Artaud attempts to destroy a history, the history of the dualistic meta-physics... the duality of the body and the soul which supports, secretly of course, the duality of speech and existence, of the text and the body, etc.[24]

In his essay "From Work to Text" Barthes states that "the theory of the text can only coincide with a practice of writing."[25] This is clearly not the case for Artaud. In fact, implicit in Artaud's enterprise we find the non-exclusivity of a *double-articulation*, or better yet, a *multi-articulation à la* Bergson. The body is a hieroglyphic or *a-signifying* "text" — a desiring-sign which gives rise through its gestures to alternative forms of expression. And yet Barthes has the audacity to say at the end of *The Pleasure of the Text* that it is writing — "vocal writing" — that Artaud recommends.

> If it were possible to imagine an aesthetic of textual pleasure, it would have to include: *writing aloud.* This vocal writing (which is nothing like speech) is not practiced, but it is doubtless what Artaud recommended...[26]

The problem with this interpretation of Artaud is that it places writing at the center of Artaud's enterprise when it is writing that becomes non-exclusively secondary to the gesture and the shout. Barthes, however, much to his credit, tries his best in *The Pleasure of the Text* to dissociate himself from the despotic Signifier and the Transcendental Signified, but returns to it again and again as the linguistically Oedipalized child (of Lacan) who returns to the Referent — mommy and daddy — for more authority.*

For Barthes, as for someone like Heidegger, reality is defined in terms of language, and language is held to be metaphysically autonomous and primordial. "Language speaks." And here lies the essential difference between Barthes and Artaud. For the latter it is the flesh, the body, which is "authentically" or "existentially" expressive; and it achieves its expressiveness through the *a-signification* of its *affective athleticism.*.

3

One of the important aspects of writing is the way in which it turns thoughts and concepts into repeatable and established texts. Neither Barthes nor Artaud approved of repetition. Barthes attacked the repetition of meaning in mass culture because he found such repetition to be destructive to the Text.

> The bastard form of mass culture is humiliated repetition. Content, ideological schema, the blurring of contradictions — these are repeated..."[27]

---

* Contrary to Julia Kristeva: the death of the Referent does not lead to "identification with a totalitarian leader," but to the very opposite — to an(archy). (*Desire in Language*, Columbia University Press, p. 139).

Barthes, then, held the repetition of signs to be a social phenomenon which degraded the Text by turning the Text into a stereotypic expression of bourgeois culture.

But for Artaud the case was much different. Artaud was opposed to the written Text on the very grounds that written texts made repetition possible. After all, literary masterpieces are established by repetition. That is to say, it is the repetition of reading and performance that establishes the Text as a fixed expression, or as the *Master*piece that it is. There are no materpieces in oral cultures. The Masterpiece is wholly a Western import.

In his essay "No More Masterpieces" Artaud writes:

> One of the reasons for the asphyxiating atmosphere in which we live without possible escape or remedy — and in which we all share, even the most revolutionary among us — is our respect for what has been written, formulated, painted, what has been given form, as if expression were not at last exhausted... we must have done with this idea of masterpieces...[28]

Masterpieces are like tombstones — *traces* of words we once uttered. So why repeat what has already been said as though one could recapture the freshness of the initial expression? Enough with hermeneutics!

> Let us leave textual criticism to graduate students, formal criticism to esthetes, and recognize that what has been said is not still to be said; that an expression does not have the same value twice; does not live two lives...[29]

Texts are to be read or performed once and then burnt (including this one). "We must get rid of our superstitious valuations of texts and written poetry," says Artaud. "Written poetry is worth reading once, and then should be destroyed."[30] And the mime, the dance, and the non-coded gesture should replace the meaningless repetition of the Text and the violence of repetition.

For instance, the violence performed by the "Harrow" in Kafka's "In The Penal Colony" is the result of the repetitive function of the inscribing machine itself.* The "Harrow" works by turning the body of the prisoner into an unforgetable text — or masterpiece — at the expense of the prisoner's life. But this doesn't apply to the "Harrow" alone. Most forms of punishment employ the use of repetition to "correct" behavior.** Teachers, for example, will sometimes command their "unruly" students to write something like "I shall not talk in class" a thousand times on paper. And in Ionesco's "The Lesson" we have a professor who kills his student by repeating the word "knife" over and over again.

"What is tragic," says Derrida, "is not the impossibility but the necessity of repetition."[31] This is the reason why Artaud wanted to replace the written Text with the body and the theater. The theater is the only place in the world where a gesture, once made, can never be made the same way twice."[32] The theater is the only place where one can

---

* For an interesting account of the violence of representation see Nietzsche's second essay in *The Genealogy of Morals*, wherein he attributes the violence of inscriptive repetition on the body to (1) the will to create a memory and (2) the will to make human beings calculable and reactive.

** For a fascinating look at the use of repetition in the "treatment" of sex deviants, see Sylvère Lotringer's *Overexposed* (Pantheon Books, 1988).

escape the violence of inscription which kills the the human spirit by using the *wild body* as a recording surface. This is what Jorge Amado's bodily "Gabriela" instinctively realized, and why she preferred the circus to the stuffy, hyperliterate atmosphere of the lecture room where the Text and not the body is allowed expression.[33]

So let us follow Gabriela into the theater. Let us dance! Enough with words! "The letter kills the spirit."[34] And a non-exclusive shift in emphasis is needed if we are to recover the affective expressiveness of our bodies.

THIRD PLATEAU

"...The excitement of traveling in a train to meet your lover, knowing he was traveling, just as excitedly, towards you. I used to think quite a lot about that."

"Yes!" admitted her mother, smiling sadly.

"Converging lines moving across the map! Sick with desire — hardly able to wait!"

D.M. Thomas
The White Hotel

"When we look at the *powerlessness* of the individual and the small face-to-face group in the world today and ask ourselves *why* they are powerless, we have to answer not merely that they are weak because of the vast central agglomerations of power in the modern, military industrial state, but that they are *weak because* they have surrendered their power to the state.

"...the punitive, interfering lover of order is usually so because of his own unfreedom and insecurity."

Colin Ward
Anarchy In Action

3

Towards a Non-Fascist or An(archical) Way of Life

This essay concerns itself with a certain kind of affective experience which Deleuze and Guatarri have come to call a *schizo stroll*. That is to say, the kind of affective "voyage," if you will, taken by such exceptional individuals as Hölderlin, Nietzsche, Kleist, Nerval, and Artaud. This is also the stroll of the an(archist): the stroll of someone who is light on his or her feet. Take Berenger in Ionesco's "A Stroll in the Air," for example. Berenger begins by taking a Sunday stroll and ends up becoming in the most literal sense a line of flight.

The problem facing us, however, is that we have forgotten how to be light on our feet: we have forgotten what it's like to dance like a star in the night sky. Or is it possible that perhaps we haven't even tried? Well, in any case, this is the problem addressed in this essay. And, of course, this is also the problematic addressed in *Anti-Oedipus.* So let us begin by considering *Anti-Oedipus* a how-to-book, a book for all and no one, a book which may be entered as one enters a *map:* from a multiplicity of directions. And furthermore let us agree with Foucault and call *Anti-Oedipus* a "book of ethics." For it is "ethics"—or more specifically—what it means to lead an a non-fascist way of life, which will concern us here.

This essay will therefore treat an(archy) as an attitude towards the world. And not as a "political" theory or base. It will begin where *Anti-Oedipus* begins: with a discussion of *desiring-production* and *desiring-machines;* and it will develop these concepts to demonstrate their relation to an(archy) or the an(archical) way of life.

1

Schizoanalysis begins at that point where Reich's political psychology ended. That is, it begins by trying to answer Reich's question concerning the desirability of the masses to oppress themselves. As Reich saw it, the modern fascist State has been established *not* by outside forces but rather by the masses themselves. For Reich, German fascism was successful precisely because the psychological structures of the masses coincided with those of their political leaders and their ideologies. For example, in speaking of Hitler's success, Reich put it as follows:

> The investigation of Hitler's mass psychological effect has to proceed from the proposition that a *führer*, or the champion of an idea, can be successful (...) only if his personal point of view,

his ideology, or his program bears a resemblance to the average structures of a broad category of individuals.[1]

This is a different way of looking at fascism. For it addresses itself first and foremost to the psychological structures which make it possible in the first place, and then only secondarily, does it turn to the "issue" of fascism as a subject for political discourse or theory.*

What this means psycho-politically is that State revolutions are preceded by revolutions of the mind. Pirsig in *Zen and the Art of Motorcycle Maintenance* says the following concerning revolutions:

> To tear down a factory or to revolt against a government or to avoid repair of a motorcycle because it is a system is to attack effects rather than causes; and as long as the attack is upon effects only, no change is possible. The true system, the real system, is our present construction of systematic thought itself, rationality itself, and if a factory is torn down but the rationality which produced it is left standing, then, that rationality will simply produce another factory. If a revolution destroys a systematic government, but the systematic patterns of thought that produced that government are left

---

* Plato already understood this in the 5th century. One may very well read *The Republic* as the first book on political psychology. What concerned Plato was the relation between the psyche and the State. In other words, the socio-political management of his fellow Greeks' *flows of desire*. See Foucualt's *The Use of Pleasure* (Pantheon Books, New York).

intact, then those patterns will repeat themselves in the succeeding government. There's much talk about the system. And so little understanding.[2]

But the one thing that Reich's political psychology overlooked was the place of desire in the fascist personality. And it is at this point that schizoanalysis and an(archy) begin. Yet, they begin with a whole new view of desire, i.e., they posit desire as active rather than reactive.

Desire for Deleuze and Guattari is always productive. It is an active, non-referential linear flow very similar to that experienced by Artaud; and doubtless, this is what Artaud had in mind when he spoke of *affective athleticism*. There is no lack here. What there is is *production:* desire producing desire, energy producing energy, and capital producing capital as it happens in capitalist society.

> As Marx notes, what exists in fact is not lack, but passion, as a "natural and sensous object." Desire is not bolstered by needs, but rather the contrary; needs are derived from desire: they are the counterproducts within the real that desire produces. Lack is a countereffect of desire; it is deposited, distributed, vacuolized within a real that is natural and social.[3]

Thus desire manifests itself at the molecular level, at the libidinal level, at the *orgone* level, at the active level, where one produces a flow as oppposed to a series of sporadic and regimented squirts. The an(archist) is he or she whose active desire is not regimented, not hier(archized) by family, church, school, army, work, etc. Let us say, then, that in essence, an an(archist) is an unstructured body, a *body w/o organs*.

But perhaps we are getting a bit ahead of ourselves. As we just said above, desire like capital should be understood in terms of flows, as for instance, flows of shit, flows of semen, flows of desire, etc. However, there is a catch here. While the *flows of desire* emanate (in a non-originary manner) from a body w/o organs, the flows of capital emanate from a hier(archical) and *arborescent* body, i.e., from the coded body of the Capitalist Socius. And a double process operates at the molar level of the economic system itself. In other words, capitalism works by inscribing, coding and re-directing the flows of desire so that they may correspond with the flows of capital at the stock market. This double process is the process of *deterritorialization* (degrounding) and *territorialization* (grounding). Desire is first *deterritorialized* by capital: allowing certain aspects of the schizophrenic process to manifest themselves, and then it *territorializes* them: whenever there is some danger that these flows may take their own *lines of flight*. Which is to say, whenever an an(archical) or *rhizomatic* act is possible. Capitalism "can only exist by liberating generic production while at the same time containing it within well-defined limits so that it doesn't flee in all directions and escape everywhere."[4]

The Film Forum in New York City plays anti-establishment and communist propaganda films, despite the fact that one of its funders is Exxon. Why? Because even though Exxon allows the release of certain an(archical) flows of desire, it can just as easily put an end to them at a well-defined point. Exxon will allow you to open your mouth and shout, but it will also shut it the moment it funds a revolution in Central America. It will fund a leftist film on Nicaragua at the very same moment that it will contribute money to further the oppression of the Nicaraguan people by a fascist leader. In New York City people who sell things on the streets are often made to close down by the police. The system will allow and even encourage the flows as long as those flows are regimented and coded. The street vendor is a threat because he steps out of the system: because he has taken to the streets "without a license," without the baptism of the system. The cop who closes down the street vendor is nothing more than the monkey wrench who puts an end to the unrestricted and noncoded flows. "The monarch of the mind," says Miller, "is a monkey wrench."[5] We may add, so is the "monarch of desire."

And yet the system not only works by a subtle subtraction but also by a subtle addition—by an axiomatic.

> The strength of capitalism resides in the fact that its axiomatic is never saturated, that it is always capable of adding a new axiom to the previous ones.[6]

Capitalism then appropriates whatever it finds to be a threat. It does this by grounding whatever is free-flowing and marginal. EMI, the British recording company, produced the "Sex Pistols" not because the executives at "the" company liked them but rather because it was easy to turn them into a commodity (an "unlimited supply"), and strip them of what little threat they may have posed to the system. "Punk" was finished the moment it became a movement with its own *signifying* semiotic and its own language and dress code.

Today one finds grandmothers everywhere with the "punk look" the same way one found the "existentialist look" in the pseudo-intellectuals of Paris in the 1950s.

As the subculture begins to strike its own emi-
nently marketable pose, as its vocabulary (both
visual and verbal) becomes more and more
familiar, so the referential context to which it
can be most coveniently assigned is made in-
creasingly apparent. Eventually the mods, the
punks, the glitter rockers can be incorporated,*
brought back into line, located on the preferred
"map of the problematic and social reality"
(Geertz, 1964) at that point where boys in lip-
stick are "just kids dressing up," where girls in
rubber dresses are "daughters just like yours..."
The media, as Stuart Hall (1977) has argued,
not only record resistance, they "situate it within
the dominant framework of meaning," and
people who choose to inhabit a spectacular
youth culture are simultaneously *returned*, as
they are represented on T.V. and in the news-
papers, to the place where common sense would
have them fit . . . [7]

Capitalism is able to function axiomatically because
the so-called "marginal language" eventually becomes established, codified, and semiotically signifying. The only way to
solve this problem is for the an(archist) to destroy his or her
own form of expression immediately, so as to make repetition and incorporation impossible.

This is partly what Artaud had in mind when he called
for the end of masterpieces — or written texts. What he

---

* "Incorporate: to form into a body (*corpus*, a body)." (*Webster's New Twentieth
  Century Dictionary*). That which is rhizomatic or an(archic) is brought into the
  body of the Socius — is formed into a body.

wanted —in the language of Guattari — was an a-signifying semiotic:[8] a flow of non-repeatable signs that would make it impossible for the system (or culture), or in this case capitalism, to incorporate them or bring them into its own body. "Anything that stands for more than ten seconds is evil," says the lyrics of a song by the punk group "Black Flag." And one finds the same idea in Ionesco's "The Lesson," where one of the characters is killed by her professor who keeps repeating the word "knife" over and over again. This is also how Kafka's despotic machine (the "Harrow") works. This process of overcoding stems from the State's fear of unrestricted desire, and certainly from capitalism's fear of certain types of *desiring-machines*. And so it employs an arrangement of fascist desiring-machines to regiment and monitor the an(archical) desiring-machines.

2

Now, we must understand *desiring-machines* within a nonexclusive context. That is to say, we must understand them as negative or fascist machines of repression, as reactive machines, as well as positive or an(archical) machines — unregimented and free-flowing. But what right do we have, you may ask, to call human beings "machines" — or even "desiring-machines"? Did we not leave those concepts behind with Descartes and Hobbes? Yes and No. We only left them behind insofar as we are no longer compelled to view machines in binary opposition to a life process (vitalism).

Machines should be understood in connection with *desiring-production*: with active desire, with desire as the kind of energy that all machines produce, from a motorcycle to a human being. "Man is sick because he is badly constructed," writes Artaud.[3] And Henry Miller writes:

> Every man, woman, and child in a mocking-
> tosh has adenoids, spreads catarrh, diabetes,
> whooping cough, meningitis. Everything that
> stands upright, that slides, rolls, tumbles, spins,
> shoots, teeters, sways and crumbles is made of
> nuts and bolts.[10]

And desiring-machines work by slowing down, breaking down, starting over, coughing, shitting, fucking, pissing, etc.

> Desiring-machines... continually break down as
> they run, and in fact, run only when they are
> not functioning properly: the product is always
> an offshoot of production, implanting itself
> upon it like a graft, and at the same time, the
> parts of the machine are the fuel that makes it
> run.[11]

Now, there are basically two types of machines. One, the *desiring-machines* which we have dealt with here. And two, the *technical machines* we deal with on a day-to-day basis — like Pirsig's motorcycle. So let us consider Pirsig and his motorcycle together, and let us call Pirsig a *desiring-machine*, and his motorcycle a *technical machine*. And furthermore let us understand that what differentiates technical machines from desiring-machines is not their size or structure, but their use. Or, as Deleuze and Guattari put it, their "regime."[12]

Chaplin, in the midst of the machine, can become either an an(archic) machine or a despotic machine or an infernal desiring-machine, becoming attached to the technical machine, as a tool of capitalist *anti-production* and technology.

> Technology presuposes social machines and
> desiring-machines, each within the other, and
> by itself, has no power to decide which will be
> the engineering agency, desire or the oppres-
> sion of desire.[13]

It is left open to Chaplin to use the monkey-wrench,
either to re-adjust (territorialize) the despotic or technical
machine of oppression, or to let loose its nuts and bolts that
like a "schizophrenic shirt"[14] are tied far too tight around his
neck. It is up to Chaplin to deterritorialize the flows of desire. In brief, then, the manner in which one plugs into another machine determines the outcome of desire. The German proletariat that put Hitler in power, that desired Hitler's
despotic machine, were able to be effective because they
plugged themselves into a despotic desiring-machine — but
a "desiring-machine" nonetheless. Moreover, desiring-machines may work both as an(archic) partial objects or as
hier(archichal) partial objects: as oppressive machines connected to other oppressive machines. Pirsig coupled to his
motorcycle is a true desiring-machine, a true an(archist), a
partial object, in the positive sense of the word. This is also
what Bukowski's and Acker's literary machines are about.
That is, an(archic) desiring-machines desiring other an(archic)
desiring machines... desire desiring desire.

On the other hand, we can find despotic desiring-machines. Kleist's *Prince Friedrich of Homburg* is a good case in
point. The Prince is a desiring-machine coupled to a despotic
or hier(archical) machine. In fact, the Prince surrenders to
the Law of the State in much the same way that the neurotic
surrenders himself or herself to the Oedipal Law. The Prince's

identity is only made possible in a triadic relationship: that of himself, the Elector (the mediator of the Law), and the State. Mommy plays the role of the State, Daddy the punishing mediator. It is only after completely surrendering to the State, to the Law, to the despotic machine, to the overcoding machine, that the Prince can at last be foregiven by the Elector, the Father.* Furthermore, we must remember that even though the Prince was a hero for having defeated the Swedes, the State nevertheless found itself obligated to sentence him to death for having disobeyed his *orders*, his *superiors*, the Law, and for having taken a line of flight, for having taken a schizo stroll, for having become a temporary an(archist), a true desiring-machine and body without organs.

Desiring-machines work at the molecular level, at the microphysical level. Contradistinctly, the socius works at the molar level, at the level of *technical machines* of repression and oppression. And just as President Schreber was plugged in to a despotic machine, so was Kleist's Prince. In both cases, the coupling occurred at the molar and hier(archical) level.

3

At the molecular level, one finds the schizophrenic process, the line of flight, and the flows of desire. Nerval takes a schizo stroll in search of "Aurelia" and ends up hallucinating his own world, painting the world his own color, in

---

* One finds the same surrender in Kafka's "The Judgment," wherein the son (Georg) is destroyed by completely surrendering to the despotic Law of the Father — in the Name of the Father.

much the same way as the Pink Panther who paints the entire world pink.[15] And in both the Pink Panther and Nerval resides the an(archist) *par excellence:* Deleuze and Guattari's body without organs and Nietzche's "self-propelled wheel."

The an(archist) is a body without organs who needs no one to determine his or her existence. In essence, an an(archist) is someone like Berenger (*Rhinoceros*), who is forever destined to remain *moving,* forever destined to remain (internally) active. "The great affair is to move," said Robert Louis Stevenson, uttering the maxim of every an(archist).

But let us be clear about this. Not every kind of movement is an(archical). It is speed which turns points into lines.

> When Glenn Gould speeds up the performance
> of a piece, he is not simply being a virtuoso; he
> is transforming the musical points into lines,
> and making the ensemble proliferate.[16]

And when Seicho Matusomoto's Detective Torigai (*Points and Lines*) sets out to solve the murder of a prominent official he does so by turning the points of a train schedule into lines of flight of an airplane trajectory. "I've got it!" he says. By plane the murderer could "leave Hakata at 8 A.M. and arrive at Sapporo at four in the afternoon."

Contrary to Paul Virilio, then, speed itself is not violence. In fact, the opposite may very easily be true. The State, the slowest of all machines, works precisely by being slow. It works best when its speed is near zero. Speed leads to chaos — a certain kind of chaos — and change, whereas order and slowness lead to a static position (a point) and a structure. Richard Sennett (*The Uses of Disorder*), like the Sex Pistols, finds the city to be the only place where an(archy) is pos-

sible, for it is here that we find the movement and Nietzschean chaos that is needed to lead an an(archical) and non-
fascist life. The an(archist) is a nomad — a nomadic desiring
machine that plugs himself/herself into other desiring-machines: never remaining dependent on any one desiring-machine in particular. Part objects (Melanie Klein) are important
for him or her only as points of connections leading to lines
of intensities: to thousands of plateaus, to thousands of
affective states.

The an(archist's) relationship with others is an active
relationship. He neither treats others as receptacles nor allows
himself to be treated as a receptacle for others. His/her connections are always binary* but never parallel. She never
belongs to a party, a nation, or any other kind of tribal alliance. She's always moving.** And she never remains in any
one place long enough to be made a "citizen" (to be territorialized). The an(archist) creates himself or herself everyday,
from scratch.

As Artaud put it: "I, Antonin Artaud, am my son, and
my father, my mother, my self..."[17] Similarly, Nietzche uttered:

> I am Prado, I am also Prado's father. I venture
> to say that I am also Lesseps... I wanted to give
> my Parisians, whom I love, a new idea — that
> of a decent criminal. I am also Chambige —
> also a decent criminal... The unpleasant thing,

---

* "Desiring-machines are binary machines, obeying a binary law or set of
  rules governing associations: one machine is always couple with another." (*Anti-Oedipus*, p. 5).

** Always "on the road," like Jack Kerouac.

and one that nags at my modesty, is that at
root every name in history is I.[18]

I, says Nietzche, am the world, and I am such because
in creating myself I create the world.

However, let us be careful here: for it is important
that we do not interepret Nietzsche as proposing some kind
of raving individualism. When Nietzsche says "I" and even
when Artaud says "I" the "I" of which they speak, the "I"
which they utter, is the "I" of rhizomatic, an(archical) relationships. Not the "I" of a paranoiac or a fascist, subjugating
others. What concerned Nietzsche above all was the possibility of affective connections between all kinds of human beings.
And what he asked from human beings themselves is that
they be as affectively intense as they could possibly be. Even
his writing style betrays this longing for a rhizomatically
intense life.

We can easily understand his aphorisms not as conceptual fragments reflecting a conceptual, non-emotive, non-
passionate life, but as plateaus... as lines of intensity which
connect at no specific place but everywhere. When Nietzsche
says that he's Prado, Prado's father, Chambige, Cesare Bor-
gia and ultimately the world what he's doing is (1) creating a
world and (2) connecting with that world affectively.

It is a question of... identifying races, cultures,
and gods with fields of intensity on the body
without organs, identifying personages with
states that will fill these fields, and with effects
that fulgurate within and traverse these fields.[19]

There is no Oedipus here. So it is not a matter of
identifying with some kind of Father figure. Instead, it is

matter of "creating" worlds and individuals in order to connect with them as fields of intensity, affectively. (Children do this all the time with their "cartoon idols," and it's not because they're looking for a Father or Mommy figure). The an(archist's) desire is not a circular, referential desire, but a linear desire.

4

In Godard's "Alphaville," the signs of violence and State oppression are circular (e.g., the emblem in the police cars).* Conradistinctly, the signs of freedom and escape (as in a line of flight or escape) are linear. That's because an(archy) manifests itself at the linear level... at the level of flight... at the molecular level... at the quantum physical level... at the subatomic level. The circle, however, is a closed geometrical figure, and therefore a symbol (and sometimes even an instrument) of oppression and repression: of boundaries and limits, and of referentiality. The an(archist), therefore, is someone who does *not* lead his or her life according to some universal Referent: according to a rigidly segmented set of boundaries and territorialities. Instead, he or she is someone who actively creates his or her own world every morning afresh.

Eldridge Cleaver, writing in *Soul on Ice*, says that that there came a point in his life when he could no longer believe in the "knowledge" of those whom he had considered above him. "I had thought," he says,

---

* Another example of the violence of circularity is found in the panopticon that Foucault talks about in *Discipline and Punish* (Vintage Books, N.Y.).

that, out there beyond the horizon of my own
ignorance, unanimity existed, that even though
I myself didn't know what was happening in
the universe, other people certainly did. Yet
there I was discovering that the whole U.S.A.
was in chaos of disagreement over segregation/
integration. In these circumstances I decided
that the only safe thing for me to do was go for
myself. It became clear that it was possible for
me to take the initiative: instead of simply re-
acting I could act. I could unilaterally —
whether anyone agreed with me or not — re-
pudiate all allegiances, morals, values — even
while continuing to exist within this society.[20]

Now here you have someone who, without ever having read a word of Nietzsche, is more Nietzschean, i.e., more
an(archical), than any academic, Nietzschean scholar.

An(archy) cannot be taught. It is not a theory. It is a way
of life, a way of being in the world, an attitude. Sylvère
Lotringer is an an(archist). The Italian "autonomists" are
an(archists). And the Rastafarians, with their own language
(*patois*) and lifestyle, are also an(archists). An(archy) takes as
many forms as there are individuals.

Anti-Oedipus is a Nietzschean book of ethics in that it
is written for all and no one simultaneously. This is why
Deleuze, in a letter to one of his critics, says that they —
meaning himself and Guattari — do not care what we as
individuals do with *Anti-Oedipus*. "We consider a book,"
writes Deleuze,

as a small a-signifying machine: the only problem is — Does it work and how does it work?

How does it work for you? If it doesn't function, if nothing happens, take another book. This other way of reading is based on intensities: something happens or doesn't happen. There is nothing to explain, nothing to understand, nothing to interpret. It can be compared to an electrical connection. A body without organs: I know uneducated people who understood this immediately, thanks to their own "habits."[21]

In a word, it all comes down to what kind affective connections we can make with the world at large. Can we still be light on our feet? Can we dance? And then: can we dance with others? Are we still capable of taking afternoon strolls with other desiring-machines? Berenger tried. He really did. But his family would not fly with him.

Someone asked me recently what my definition of an(archy) was. I had no response: because an(archy) is life.

FOURTH

PLATEAU

BEFORE TAKE-OFF

(1) Cabin Doors — LATCHED.
(2) Flight Controls — FREE AND CORRECT.
(3) Elevator Trim — TAKE-OFF.
(4) Fuel Shutoff Valve — ON.
(5) Brakes — SET.
(6) Throttle — 1700 RPM.
    (a) Magnetos—CHECK (RPM drop should not
    exceed 150 RPM on either magneto or 75
    RPM differential between magnetos).
    (b) Carburetor Heat — CHECK (for RPM drop).
    (c) Engine Instruments & Ammeter —CHECK.
    (d) Suction Gage — CHECK.
(7) Flight Instruments and Radios — SET
(8) Throttle Friction Lock — ADJUST.
(9) Wing Flaps — 0 degrees.

TAKE-OFF

(1) Wing Flaps — 0 degrees.
(2) Carburetor Heat — COLD.
(3) Throttle — FULL OPEN.
(4) Elevator Control—LIFT NOSE WHEEL (55 MPH).
(5) Climb Speed — 70–80 MPH.

Instructions from *The Owner's Manual*
of a 1975 Cessna 150.

We work week in and week out. Until each one of the four of us sympathetically feels what the other one is doing, without ever saying it... Each of us just link, just gradually link together as a component of a huge machine. And that's what we always strive for. Later you can put little breaks into it, and structure it by putting points of interest in. But the basic thing is always the same-it's just four people striving to get the hugest... striving to get bigger and harder, until those wheels just come down harder!!!

Test Department, Interview in "Terminal"
by Andy Darlington (No. 16/17)

4

MOLECULAR REVOLUTION, ART AND AN(ARCHY)

Processes everywhere, the dynamic flows of subatomic interactions, chemical flows — all processes, all an(archic) processes emanating from everywhere... like the flows in Bergson's *Creative Evolution*, Freud's libido, Reich's orgone energy, Monod's DNA, etc., etc. And then, of course, the flows of desire of artists and their art:* their passion, their schizo strolls, which are again, an(archic) flows of desire, lines of flight, as for example the lines of flight found in the harsh brush strokes of Van Gogh and Bacon, and in the photographic plates depicting subatomic interactions.

And yet, what has any of this to do with art and an(archy)? What do we mean by molecular revolution? Is it

---

* By the word "art," we mean to include here not only visual art or painting, but also poetry, literature, music, film, etc. And the same applies to the word "artist."

another Ivory Tower term? After all, how do we connect the DNA code to the State, to the fascist body, to the body infected with organs (or micro-powers)?

A mere madness? But then, of course, we know better than to call this or that "mad" as opposed to "sane." Don't we? We no longer believe in categories, fuck Aristotle! If Nietzsche and Derrida have shown us anything, it is that there is no longer a solitary and absolute position to hold, but a multiplicity of positions, constantly in flux. These molecular flows, these flows of desire, are *a-topic*, i.e., they are nomadic and without a place. If we could localize them, they would immediately become points: States, churches, dictators, dogmas, ideologies, etc. No, we want none of that. That which is static is violent and oppressive, and we have had our fill of both. This essay will find as its concern the connections to be made, here and there, between the molecular flows and the flows of desire found in an(archic) artists and their art.

1

"The biologist who makes a model of the RNA and DNA chains is transposing these structures into a system of signs, thus producing an entirely new basis of expression," says Guattari in *Molecular Revolution*.[1] And we find this to be the case with someone like Jacques Monod. For Monod the DNA code is an invariant, territorializing structure, as of course, all structures are. In fact, the different varieties of biological organisms in nature are the result of such an invariance in the DNA code. M. Monod proposes that chance and necessity are not exclusive binary opposites, but in rather non-exclusive laws of nature.

The universal components — the nucleotides on the one side, the amino acids on the other — are the logical equivalents of an alphabet in which the structure and consequently the specific associative functions of proteins are spelled out. In this alphabet can therefore be written all the diversity of structures and performances the biosphere contains. More, with each succeeding cellular generation it is the *ne varietur* reproduction of the text, written in the form of DNA nucleotide sequences, that guarantees the invariance of the species...[2] (Monod's italics).

However, the apparent an(archy) of chance in Monod's DNA code is just that — apparent. The seemingly free molecular flows are anything but free; they belong to a hier(archy) in which the despotic DNA determines the outcome. One can clearly see the Hegelian–Marxist influence here, which is to say, the all-encompassing overdetermination of all the elements absorbed, and carried "forward" by Absolute Reason. The only difference is that Monod calls Absolute Reason by a different name — or more precisely, DNA. In any case, Monod's molecular flows are made fascist under the banner of liberal socialism... which turns every flow, and every line of flight into a State. And let us not be fooled by rhetoric: it is a lie to say that there exists or can exist temporary States, which later turn into flows and lines of flight — even if these States are called "proletarian States."

Furthermore, the invariance of the DNA structure is made possible only by appealing to what is easiest for Reason to understand. Monod remarks:

> It may be asked, of course, whether all the in-
> variant, conservations, and symmetries that
> make up the texture of scientific discourse are
> not fictions substituted for reality in order to
> obtain a workable image of it — an image par-
> tially emptied of substance, but accessible to
> the operations of a logic itself founded on a
> purely abstract "conventional" principle of
> identity — a convention which, however, hu-
> man reason seems incapable of doing with-
> out.*3

Thus, Monod appeals to Reason for support of his
invariance theory. And in this respect, Monod's theory of
invariance resembles Chomsky's. In effect, Monod himself
says the following:

> According to Chomsky and his school, in-
> depth linguistic analysis reveals, beneath their
> boundless diversity, one basic "form" common
> to all languages. Therefore Chomsky feels this
> form must be considered *innate* and character-
> istic of the species. Certain philosophers or an-
> thropologists have been scandalized by this
> thesis, in it discerning a return to Cartesian
> metaphysics. Provided its implicit biological

---

* A good example of asymmetry is the exclusive left-handedness of neutrinos. As Chen Yang and Tsung Dao Lee have proved, neutrinos
have only a left-handed spin, a fact that violates the parity conserva-
tion theory of nature. For an interesting discussion on this topic, see
Heinz R. Pagels', *The Cosmic Code* (Bantam Books, 217-218).

content be accepted I see nothing wrong with it whatsoever.[4] (Monod's italics)

And further down:

If these are correct assumptions, the linguistic capacity that declares itself in the course of the brain's epigenetic development is today part of "human nature," itself defined within the genome in the radically different language of the *genetic* code.[5] (my italics)

Furthermore, one can easily find a one-to-one correspondence between their theories of invariance and their political views. For Chomsky, his theory of linguistic invariance, or what he calls "universal generative grammar," allows for the range in which "uncaused," creative, linguistic competence is to be found.

But as Deleuze and Guattari have pointed out, Chomsky's universal generative grammar (like Monod's invariant DNA code) is a source of power, and authority — a fascist machine, so to speak.

The grammaticality of Chomsky, the categorical symbol S, is first a marker of power before being a syntactic marker: you will form grammatically correct sentences, you will separate each statement into a nominal syntagm and a verbal syntagm (the first dichotomy).[6]

And, of course, you will read and write as told. Therefore, what you have here is a despotic Structure which determines the direction and flow of all the elements within its regime.

Moreover, notice whence both Monod and Noam Chomsky argue their points. We do not need a magnifying glass to see that what is fundamentally at stake here is the old Platonic–Kantian Reason again. In both Monod's DNA and in Chomsky's generative grammar, we find a hier-(archy) (the tree and the chain) in which the free-flowing elements within their respective Structures are regulated and channeled: (1) you will write as such, and *only* as such, and (2) you will understand creation in terms of Code, and *only* in terms of Code. As such, Chomsky territorializes the flow of words, and Monod territorializes the genetic flows.

In either case, Plato's Rational part of the soul is duplicated in a somewhat different mold. The free-flowing flows of desire and lines of flight are regimented and controlled by both Monod and Chomsky, in a manner similar to Plato's. That is, the flows of desire, the molecular flows, etc., are all subsumed under paranoiac, insomniac Reason. Zeus will not be allowed to fuck Hera on the steps of the temple... he will have to wait until he's inside. Restrain yourself, man! The DNA's despotic nature will determine the outcome of everything; and most clearly, there will be no disorder, but only hier(archical) organization.

It is irrelevant whether we find the hier(archy) in the tree or in the chain. In the end, the tree and the chain amount to the same — namely, Reason. The employment of too many strings in an instrument leads to an(archy), says Plato in *The Republic*. Music must be ordered and harmonious, there must be no dissonance or discord. In answer to the One/Many problem, Plato chose the One over the Many, and Being over Becoming. And two thousand years later, we encounter the same move in Monod and Chomsky, the only difference is that Being and the One have been given different names — namely, DNA and generative grammar. The

One is Reason: the guiding Structure of all structures, the Structures that makes it possible to see the world in terms of structures. And what is the Many? The many is the non-originary instincts: the passions, desires, etc., all that is nomadic and *a-topic*: all that is free-flowing and non-localizable, lines instead of points, movement instead of states.

As Bergson pointed out, we deal with "states" only because Reason needs to freeze movement in order to understand the phenomenon. Movement does not correspond to Reason, but to the affects, to *flows of desires*, to *desiring-production*, to the passions, which are always active. If Monod and Chomsky tell you that creativity is possible in necessity, that chance is possible in necessity, that freedom is possible in a universal Structure, don't you believe it — at least, not any more than you should believe that freedom is possible in a political State. Let us not forget that a state is simply a *frozen* moment. And a moment frozen by Reason in order to keep all the elements within it manageable, coded, and of course, fixed.

Camus, for example, was well aware of the fact that the State works through Reason, and that State oppression is always the result of Reason.* And, as Lyotard remarks in *Driftworks*:

> Reason and power are one and the same thing. You may disguise the one with dialectics or prospectiveness, but you will still have the other in all its crudeness: jails, taboos, public weal, selection, genocide.[7]

---

* For an accurate and interesting critical treatment of Reason and the mathematics and logic of State oppression, see Albert Camus' "Caligula" and "State of Siege" (*Caligula and Three Other Plays*) (Vintage Books).

Too many strings? That is a problem! How does one code the multiplicity of strings, of flows? How does one territorialize (or ground) the desires in such a way so that they remain subservient to the Master, Reason? Perhaps the installation of a territorializing machine is the answer, as for example, Plato's educational machine. Plato's machine worked, first by *deterritorializing* the passions (yes, you may fuck if you want), and secondly by *reterritorializing* them at a certain point (no, you may not fuck Hera on the steps to the temple). All is well as long as the territorializing machine is in place, as long as the content is there; which is to say, the DNA code, universal generative grammar, dialectic, Absolute Knowledge, noumena, phenomena, the Transcendental Signfied, God, etc., etc.

The non-coded flows of desire must be turned into referential and signifying units and they must be made to refer back to a content, to an authority, call it DNA, universal grammar, or Oedipus. In any case, order must be imposed. (Words must correspond to things in the world, as in Foucault's *Les mots et les choses*, they must not be a-signifying, as in the case of Burroughs or e.e. cummings). Yes, music as expression must have a content, it must not be random, atonal, or dysfunctional, it must refer back to some ordering sign, just as the different varieties of biological organisms in the biosphere must refer back to the DNA code. Random notes, dysfunctional music, and asignifying expression, are the enemies of authority. After all, what if there is no Oedipus, no DNA code, no generative grammar, what if there is no God, no Horizon, no Referent, asks the paranoiac trembling. And Hobbes answers. Molecular flows must be regimented for the paranoiac. To live in the post-modern world, which is to say in a Nietzschean world, one must be brave enough to sail in a vast ocean whose horizon has been wiped away by a sponge. These men — Chomsky and Monod — are afraid to navigate without a compass. Analytic philosophy, cognitive psychology, behaviorism — all these are after-effects of the death of the Referent. And the kind of art which results from such fear is fascist art: art in which the *flows of desire* are *represented*, circularized, and regimented.

The moment that art and artists become *a-signifying* they become free and independent of any hier(archical) framework. *A-signifying* art is one of the many manifestations of *desiring-production*.

> Desire does not "want" revolution, it is revolutionary in its own right, as though involuntarily, by wanting what it wants.[8]

Thus desiring production, or active desire, is a threat to the body infected with organs (or contents) and an(archic) art, being a manifestation of such, is also a threat. In fact, true "revolutionary art" does not even call itself by that name, for to do so is to give itself a name, a referent, a localizable point, an origin... all that is reactive as opposed to active and free. An(archic) art is precisely that because it refuses to call itself by any name. So-called an(archic) art is one of the many manifestations of active desire. It does not react to a Structure, it does not refer back to an authority, it is a flow of desire, like the free molecular flow without the invariance of the DNA code. Or, in the language of Chomsky, a language without a *universal generative grammar*.

2

All these processes, all these molecular flows take place on the body without organs, on the plane of consistency (*Mille Plateaux*). And yet certain of these molecular flows are arrested by molar aggregates, and grounded to the body infected with organs, to the fascist body. The deformed infant in *Eraserhead* is an arrangement of organs without a body: the product of a bad connection made between two desiring-machines. The semi-formed embryos squashed by the monstrous singing woman… an inferno of desire, and meanwhile the sounds of fascist industrial machines in the background — the same machines that one also encounters in David Lynch's later film, *The Elephant Man*. Again, the monstrosity occurs at the molar level, at the level of the organs, not the body. The infant is deformed because *it* does not have a body. Instead, it has its organs wrapped inside a small sheet of cloth. David Lynch is concerned with the organs attached to the body: the tumors of the singing woman in *Eraserhead*, the tumors of John Merrick in *The Elephant Man*, and finally, a body of flows in his film version of Frank Herbert's *Dune*. Here at last we have a desert instead of industrial machines… a body without organs to be crossed, and flows (of water) to be released. The despot comes from the desert to territorialize the flows on the body — and in the end we even have a certain kind of profit. Or more precisely, here we encounter an economy, like capitalism, in which the flows of water instead of the flows of capital are territorialized. (Schizophrenia is arrested as a process, and turned into a state.) The flows of desire are guided and channeled in a certain direction. They are made to conform to a referent. And again, here we encounter the most heinous kind of violence and perversion. Here monstrosity takes root. The tube connected between two anuses in Michael Gira's "Some Weaknesses," is the perfect example.

> When one of us takes a shit, the pressure builds in the tube and the shit slowly works its way up the others' ass. She's berating me. (I can tell by the expression of hunger-anger on her face) for not shitting more often. She wants my shit up her ass. I have the ability to hold it in. She knows this. That's why she plugged my mouth and ears, so it would eventually have to come out of my ass. But I won't. Right now I can feel it crawling up my throat, and it's going to start coming out of my nostrils any second, first in slow drips, then in a quick brown double-stream I'll aim at her ugly, selfish face.[9]

Q.: And what is this all about? A.: A connection between two desiring-machines who wish to have their flows grounded to something — anything. Yes, shit will flow, but it will have its destination. In Gira's case, the destination is the mouth and the nostrils. (In the language of psychoanalysis, the old problem of "anal retention," finds here a partial answer.) In any case, the flows we encounter in Gira are different from the flows we encounter in Beckett. The mouth in "Not I" speaks without a referent, without a signified, or content. Here we have free flows of words and desires. When it screams, it shakes our very being because it is a voice that travels out into space, out into the desert, and crosses the body without organs never to return again. It is a voice forever travelling. And yes, it is a terrifying voice, and a terrifying mouth because of its solitariness. On the other hand, while Gira's mouth disgusts us, it does not make us tremble... we see the tube which connects A to B, but where's the larynx in Beckett's mouth? Beckett's mouth is the mouth of the nomad who shouts in the middle of the desert. It is not a voice that aims at anything in particular, but simply a voice — a terrifying voice; the same voice we hear when we listen to recordings of Artaud chanting — a voice that is not so much a voice as a sound, and a very "cruel" sound at that. It is a disturbing sound for we do not know whence it comes, and where its headed. In any case, what is at stake here is the asignification of the voice, i.e., its an(archic) nature, and its non-referential possibilities.

The problem concerning an(archic) expression comes in when the voice is connected or coupled to a social organism, that is to say, to an established language with its own invariant (DNA) code and universal generative grammar.* For example, the youth gang in Anthony Burgess' *A Clockwork Orange* is a micro-fascist group, precisely because all it does is to substitute one code for another, or more precisely, one dress code, one linguistic code for another, and hence all it replaces is one system of signification, one universal generative grammar for another. In short, the micro-fascist youth gang in Burgess' *A Clockwork Orange* remains within its own signifying semiotic register; and as much a part of the established code as the police. The police are able to deprogram Alex because all they have to do is simply invert the code to read its opposite, a simple enough project when

---

* This is precisely why someone like Eco is a fascist: his theory of code production is a theory of (fascistic) linguistic invariance, which makes rebellion against the established order or code impossible. For Eco one must always remain a model reader, and never a scrambler of codes.

the code is merely transferred from one side of the / to the other, from disobedience to obedience, from disrespect to respect, from desire to lack of desire, and so on. All that was needed in the case of Alex was a simple device to force the eyes to remain open.

The problem here is the body as limit, the body as wall, and of course, the body as Structure — as in Kafka's "The Great Wall of China." One needs to break walls, to shatter them to bits, but never to wail before them. The impact of a body hitting a wall always creates another casualty, another Hölderlin, another Nietzsche, another Artaud, another Van Gogh, etc. Too many casualties! And the wall, of course, is always a limit, whether it be language, God, mommy, daddy, Oedipus, or anything else. Casualties occur sometimes even at the end of a stroll, perhaps even as a result of a woman (called "Aurelia"), or an Egyptian queen, as with Nerval. Why is it that certain of these individuals like D. H. Lawrence, Henry Miller, Jack Kerouac, Allen Ginsberg, etc., never continue to cross the body without organs?[10] As Deleuze and Guattari point out in *Anti-Oedipus*, it is fear which prevents them from going all the way... fear that they may never be able to return. "The majority draw near the wall and back away horrified."[11] To take a schizo stroll, one must be willing to take a considerable chance with one's life. In brief, one must be willing to sail without a compass, to enter unexplored lands, as another Bowman in the midst of a solitary universe.

Lautréamont's "Maldoror," for example, comes close to the limit; however, in the end, he merely leaves the world of the Earth for the world of the Sea... only to create a psychopathic inversion of the former. Who cares whether God sits on a throne or on a pile of shit? Who cares for the opposition Good/Evil? We left that behind us long ago. And whether Maldoror becomes man or shark is irrelevant. In either case, men and sharks have their own codes. Maldoror's code is simply the opposite of the code "Good." It is interesting that like his French compatriot, the Marquis de Sade, all he has done is to replace one code with another. He has replaced the code of "Good" with the code of "Evil," just as de Sade replaced the bourgeois code of his day with the code of "libertinage." De Sade wanted the world to become libertine, Maldoror wanted the world to become Evil: the former wanted the world as a House of Libertinage, and the latter, the world as Sea... as a Sea of infinite blood. Both Lautréamont and de Sade wanted something to remain invariant, something to remain divine — a divinity steeped in blood perhaps, but nevertheless a divinity. In the end, they were both concerned with states of being as opposed to processes of becoming.

Moreover, they were both concerned with a *counting-body*. Maldoror was concerned with the logic and mathematics of Evil, and de Sade with the logic and mathematics of sex. The old body count: "how many have I killed?" and "how many have I fucked?" Yes, mathematics and the fascist body are always connected. The body count and the counting-body belong to the fascist formation, as for instance, Hemingway's body: the body of a paranoiac machine holding a gun in his hand, proud of his hunting trophies that sit on a table in the background — like the Logan brothers' bowling trophies.[12]

And then we have Stanley Kowalski's body... such good measurements, such good biceps.

> Now what are all these furs doing here, how about these pearl,s Stella? Where are your pearls, Stella?

He wants someone to come in and appraise Blanche's "possessions." Stanley Kowalski wants numbers, figures, he was never good in English. How could Blanche have lost Belle Reve? But poor Blanche, she knows nothing of numbers; she had simply been taking a stroll long ago, and didn't see the wall in time to avoid it. Blanche's body is not a counting-body. And Stanley, how is he to deal with a non-counting body, with a body without organs? Well, he must demarcate it, he must measure the territory, he must territorialize Blanche's flows of desire. In the state of Louisiana, there is a Napoleonic *code* that says that what belongs to the husband also belongs to the wife, and vice-versa. Napoleon, the despot, is going to make sure that he doesn't get swindled, that the mathematics are correct, and if they are not, well, poor Blanche must be put away. That is why Stanley has her taken to a mental institution. There will be no an(archic) desiring-machine here — perhaps they are contagious — that is his fear. The paranoiac must lock up the little desiring-machine from Belle Reve. There will be no processes in Stanley's territory, only states: everything must remain as it is: the bowling games, the heavy drinking, the poker game, and work at the factory. No, desiring-machines "must" not be soft, they "must" be rigid, and work exclusively within their prescribed regime. That is the reason why Stanley Kowalski tells Mitch everything about Blanche's life — he does not want another soft desiring-machine around. Machines "must" be made of metal, like Mark Pauline's destructive and fascistic desiring-machines... which he unleashes in public places: machines which in fact have hurt people.[13] These machines, these bodies, are the enemies of flows.

However, there are an(archic) bodies, and an(archic) desiring-machines, like the ones we find in the literature of

Henry Miller. His bodies are concerned with flows, with processes, and in his hand we always find a monkey wrench ready to release the flows of the body without organs, and the flows of desire. Miller's bodies are always active bodies... bodies in motion, bodies fucking away, releasing flows of sperm, ejaculating, regardless of the place. For Miller there is no sacred place for the sex act, he will fuck (Hera) anywhere, sacred places belong to paranoiacs. This is why Wyndham Lewis' "wild bodies" never seem quite wild enough — in fact, they even seem static — their wildness, their "dynamism" is always contextualized, they are wild bodies in Brittany, wild bodies in Spain, always wild bodies some place in particular, and hence, they are not wild at all. A truly wild body, a body without organs, doesn't belong to anything, it has no mommy–poppy, and no country or land that it calls its own. The body without organs is merely an undifferentiated surface, a plane of consistency, always *a-topic*. It is a surface for desiring-machines: the kind of desiring-machines we encounter in D. M. Thomas' *The White Hotel*, and their flows of milk, flows of sperm, flows of blood. And also the kind of desiring-machines we encounter in J. G. Ballard's *The Unlimited Dream Company*. Blake is a desiring-machine who begins by taking a stroll and ends up taking a line of flight: a Cessna 150 whose destination is a Dionysian world of desire where human beings become birds, where bodies become passionate, weightless, and defy the spirit of gravity. In Blake's world, there is no mommy, daddy, children, etc., as differentiated *subjects* — all we have are bodies without organs in constant motion.

3

Lines, not points, that's what we are concerned with. Unlike Georges Seurat, we define reality in terms of lines instead of points. We interpret light in terms of waves, not particles or photons. And like Charles Bukowski, we are interested only in lines. Neither his "periods" nor his "commas" belong to Chomsky's grammatical tree.* What you find in the literature of Bukowski, from his poetry to his prose, is a certain kind of rhizomatic or linear writing, in which grammaticality and structure is dismissed.

> Commas suggest relation, order, structure; here what needs to be brought out is the brute facts themselves, and they must be left as unstructured as possible.[14]

This is also the case with the poetry of John Cage, and e.e. cummings. Commas, periods, semi-colons, all these grammatical devices make affective expression impossible — they turn affectivity into linguistic expression, replacing it with the plasticity of language.

One of the first artists to have noticed this problem was Tristan Tzara. Tzara wanted expression to remain wholly affective; he wanted to leave language unadorned, unstructured, and free from the despotism of consciousness.

---

* "Government is a tree," says John Cage in X. And the tree is always a model of hier(archy) and oppression, as for example, the tree of knowledge, which as we know from Foucault is always connected to power. No, we do not want trees, but rhizomes instead. Let us not forget Robespierre's "planted trees" and want they led to.

This was the whole idea behind the dadaist movement, not to be confused with the surrealist movement. One was not interested in proper grammar, one did not care for the despotism of a universal generative grammar, one did not care about proper beginnings or proper endings... one never *began* a piece of writing, one simply entered an already moving process, and one always did so from a multiplicity of directions, the same way one enters a map.

One finds this kind of linear writing in Artaud and Bukowski. There are no beginnings or endings in the writings of Artaud and Bukowski, and certainly no orgasm or climax. The entirety of their writings are composed of plateaus, thousands of plateaus, lines of intensities, and unlike mainline literary writing they are not orgasmic; that is, they do not employ endings, but rather processes, lines of intensities, more intense than any orgasm, more intense than any climax. Life is implicit in lines, whereas death is implicit in points, in the orgasm. The orgasm is a conclusion, an end-result, a period, a point... very much like death. There is even a certain deflation in it that is easily associated with death, as for instance, the orgasm-death in Oshima's "In the Realm of the Senses." There are people who have hung themselves to achieve an orgasm. An orgasm is like the capitalist idea of a "vacation": temporary intensity, and then there is work again — or death. This is also why Nietzsche wrote aphorisms. Nietzsche was concerned with intensities, with flows of desire, with linearity, and as such, his aphorisms should be read as plateaus, as lines of intensities, and as so many manifestations of affectivity. And the same applies to La Rochefoucauld, and Basho's *haikus*: this is the proper way to read a *haiku*. But in the West, we subsume everything under Language and Reason. This is why Artaud turned to the East to practice his "affective athleticism."

Now let us take a look at Ravel's *Bolero*. Here we find an affective-machine, and a certain way of *becoming-intense* (*devenir-intense*)[15] through the increase of speed. Ravel's *Bolero* may begin either "fast" or "slow," and its duration is determined by the conductor accordingly. Thus the *Bolero* serves as a good example of what Deleuze and Guattari call *devenir-intense* or becoming-intense (*Mille Plateaux*). The problem with the *Bolero* is that it *ends* with an explosion, with a climax, with an orgasm, and as such, it is arborescent rather than rhizomatic. After all, this was the reason that the *Bolero* was used in the American sex-comedy "10." In brief, the *Bolero* resembles capitalism far too much. The flows deterritorialized in the beginning of the *Bolero* are also re-territorialized in the climactic and explosive conclusion. The process released at the beginning is arrested in the end. (Let us not forget that Ravel himself was a "failed" pilot.) This double process of deterritorialization and reterritorialization is found most explicitly in the quasi-atonality of Schoenberg's compositions. Schoenberg was never able to go all the way with his attempts at composing dissonant music. The very few times that he allowed for dissonance in his music, he only did so with the intention of grounding it to a structure in the end. As a result, every single one of his compositions remained very much within the harmonious model of musicology, and his pieces, regardless of how "dissonant" or "dysfunctional" they became, always remained within the classical *state* of harmony. In a word, he was never able to break away from Plato's musical harmonics.

In fact, Schoenberg resembles both Chomsky and Monod in that the apparent an(archy) of his compositions is just that — apparent. Schoenberg was never interested in the schizophrenia of music as a process, but rather the schizophrenia of music as a state (the harmony/dissonance dichotomy). Schoenberg believed in Structure just as much as Monod and Chomsky. He wanted flows to be regimented and channeled in a certain direction, and like Aguirre in Herzog's *Aguirre, the Wrath of God*, he wanted to be the director. Schoenberg himself said the following:

> I was continually preoccupied with the intention of *grounding* the *structure* of my music consciously on a *unifying* idea that would produce not only other ideas but also *regulate* their accompaniment and the chords, the "harmonies." (my italics)[16]

What he wanted, like Chomsky and Monod, was for something to remain invariant. It is in this respect that the music of Schoenberg resembles capitalism: the schizophrenic process implicit in dissonance is arrested and turned into a state: the flows of desire that Plato feared so much are territorialized or grounded to the body infected with organs, to the capitalist body, or, what amounts to the same, to the fascist body. Schoenberg like Plato allows us to take a schizo stroll, but never too far. He is afraid that we may attempt to escape (like Blake) in a Cessna 150 — so the only kind of stroll that he will allow us to take is a suburban Sunday stroll, a Shepperton stroll.

"A light tension is created by a tiny dissonance, and it is washed away with a tonic chord."[17] Again, this is the way capitalism works: points are turned into lines only to be turned into points again.

One finds this to be the case with the literature of Louis-Ferdinand Céline (*Guignol's Band*, for example). *Guignol's Band* is a paranoiac machine that, by showing the world as chaos, as dissonance, aims to subsume chaos and dissonance under the Rule of Law. This is what Céline craved for: a world of authority and Law. Lyotard tells us in *Driftworks* that "dysfunction creates a desire to restore to good form,"[18] and this was the reason why Céline wrote the way he wrote. Do not be fooled by his an(archic) style — he was far from being anything of the sort. His reasons for writing were not the same as those of Bukowski, as much as this may seem to be the case. Our paranoid fascist wanted *order* above all. He wanted a world which had lost its Horizon to be coded again. He craved for the resurrection of the dead Referent, whose death Nietzsche had celebrated years earlier. Bukowski, on the other hand, takes pleasure in scrambling the codes, and his writings, like those of Nietzsche, celebrate the end of our Horizon, or what may also be called the end of the old, established order.

We have had our fill with order, "we do not want more order, a music that is more tonal, more unified, more rich, more elegant. We want less order, more circulation by chance, by free wandering..."[19] That is correct, we want less elegance, we are tired of over-produced, over-written music, art, literature, etc. We want the punk music of Amaury Perez's "Amor Fati," recorded with a $15.00 mike, we want truly underground music... no reproductions please! We want a "poor music," like a "poor theater," but without any of the codes found in the latter (in Grotowski). We want music that scrambles the codes, free molecular music, music which releases the flows of desire, music which takes us places, and inspires us to take our strolls, like that of the *Sex Pistols*, *Bauhaus*, etc. Oh yes, we want fast, dissonant music... music that disturbs — metallic music even, like Nick Cave, *SPK*, *Test Dept.*, *Einstürzende Neubaten*, and *Throbbing Gristle*.[20] But let us not stop here. Everyone should make music: bang a drinking glass with a knife and fork and record it, cut a fart and record it, brush your teeth and record it — yes, all that may simply be called "noise," but noise is music. Only one must learn to listen with a third ear. Even the *Sex Pistols* tell us that what they have is noise, but so what? Let us blow Plato to smithereens.

No more harmonics please! Music, like every other kind of art should be libidinal, music should be intense, like a Pollock painting — a conflagration of colors, a multiplicity of colors, none having dominance over the others. Jazz is like that: there is no domination in it, even if it is over-coded as a kind of musical expression. Perhaps its only drawback is a certain lack of dynamism, a certain lack of Dionysian energy — the kind of Dionysian energy one finds in the harsh and deep brush strokes of Van Gogh, and I am specifically thinking of "Starry Night." We want structureless flows, and wild and passionate flows of desire. And like Blake (*The Unlimited Dream Company*) and Berenger (*A Stroll in the Air*) we want to take a flight. We want to become birds; we are interested in the process of *becoming-animal*, becoming-bird, not beetle. There are runways everywhere, one only needs to use them. Blake began by coupling with another desiring-machine (a Cessna 150) and ended up coupling with the whole town of Shepperton. The higher one flies, the easier it becomes. What prevents most people from taking Blake's flight, from taking flying lessons, is fear... fear that they may enjoy themselves, fear that they may feel alive for once. As the *Sex Pistols* tell us, for most people, "it's too much fun being alive."

We leave you then, with easy-to-follow instructions to learn how to fly. This is what molecular revolution, art and an(archy) is all about. There was never anything more to it than this. Forget Marx, Bakunin, Kropotkin and the rest: too many bearded men. And we've had it up to our necks with bearded men. These men belong to history, and we've had it with history. Fuck History, we are sick of the stench that emanates from the dead! We want a nomadology instead. We aim to move, to dance, to fly, to live!

FIFTH
PLATEAU

It is the inherited burden of being condemned to live out the role of "the Other." The fault should not be seen as existing primarily in victimized individuals, but rather in demonic power structures which induce individuals to internalize false identities.

Mary Daly
Beyond God the Father

The Women's Liberation movements are correct in saying: We are not castrated, so you get fucked.... it should be recognized that Women's Liberation movements contain, in a more or less ambiguous state, what belongs to all requirements of liberation: the force of the unconscious itself, the investment by desire of the social field, the disinvestments of repressive structures.

Gilles Deleuze & Felix Guattari
Anti-Oedipus

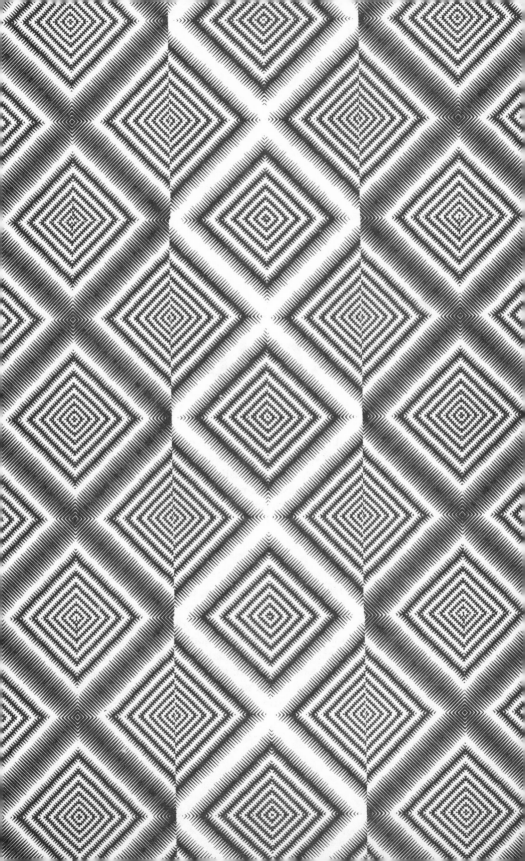

5

THE FASCISTIC STRUCTURE OF REACTIVE DESIRE, AND ITS RELATION TO THE DOMINATION OF WOMEN

For the last two thousand years, philosopher after philosopher and psychologist after psychologist (and I include Plato as the first psychologist) have told us that desire is the irrational and obsessive wish to have something we lack. And as good, obedient students and consumers of both philosophy and psychology, we have bought this view of desire unquestioningly — a view of desire which has been used from Plato to the post-modern world of advertising technologies, to control and regulate the lives of human beings, as they see fit. In brief, then, this view of desire has become a fascist tool, and a monkey wrench of oppression.

In fact, it even led earlier in this century to Hitler's "final solution." All that Hitler had to do was convince the German people that what they desired, and, of course, *lacked*, was a "clean" Germany... a Germany devoid of the "Jewish filth."

Again, what is implicit in this view, and what is important for us here, is the oppressive characteristic of *reactive desire*. For our purposes, we will concentrate on what role this view of desire plays in relation to Freud's concept of "penis envy," and the well-known "Oedipal complex," and its repressive–oppressive character. Moreover, we will provide an alternative theory of desire. That is, we will postulate desire as active and productive, as opposed to reactive and oppressive, as in Freud.

We stipulate here that this other way of understanding desire is the only revolutionary, and hence, constructive way of viewing desire. Thus, given this view of desire, i.e., *active desire*, and its feminist implications, we will also offer an alternative way of looking at human beings. For we refuse to adopt, or sanction in any way whatsoever, the old subject–object, self–other, personological model of human beings, and their relationships with each other. Instead, we offer an an(archic) view of human relationships, in which power *does not* play a role. In the language of Deleuze and Guattari, we wish to treat human beings as connecting desiring-machines, for whom relationships are not vertical and hier(archical), but horizontal and an(archical). This view is completely unlike the vertical and hier(archical) Freudian view, which finds its articulation and exemplary form in the repressive–oppressive hier(archy) of the Oedipal triangle.

1

According to Freuds' theory of "penis envy," little girls "realize," at approximately the age of three, that they "lack" something. And the full realization of what this is comes about when they compare their genitals to those of their sexual counterparts. As a result the little girls feel that they have been castrated, and they envy the uncastrated boys for having the penises they themselves lack. Their clitorises represent for them reminders of that which they do not have. In turn, they deal with this complex framework by sublimating their

> wish for a penis in the wish for a child, that is, becoming a *normal* woman, or by the development of neurosis, or by a character change described as the *masculinity complex,* *a type of character which seeks to deny that any lack exists*[1] (my italics).

Notice how normality and abnormality have been defined. A "normal" woman is defined as a woman who has accepted the "fact" that she envies and *desires* a penis; an "abnormal" woman, on the other hand, is defined as a woman who denies the "fact" that she lacks, envies, and desires a penis.

Thus, at the center of women's oppression we find a

---

* For further elucidation of the "masculinity complex," see Freud's essay, "Feminity," in the *Standard Edition* (*New Introductory Lectures on Psychoanalysis and Other Works*, ed. James Strachy, Hogarth Press).

phallocentric view of the world, grounded on reactive desire. Consequently, any woman who refuses to view the world in terms of the phallus, is held to be neurotic or highly unrealistic. Lying at the root of phallocentrism, we have what Derrida has come to call a "metaphysics of presence."

What this means for women is that reality is defined in terms of a presence/absence dichotomy, and that of course "woman" corresponds to the latter side of this division .

We find this to be the case from Plato and Aristotle to Freud and Sartre. For Plato, woman represented the appetitive and inferior part of the soul, which needed to be subordinated to the superior, Rational part of the soul, since woman lacked Reason. In fact, in the allegory of the "timocratic man" (Book VIII), Plato blames the young man's mother for being a bad influence on her son. The young man's father, on the other hand, is portrayed as a Rational man who cares neither for honors nor for wealth.[2]

Now, for Aristotle, as Caroline Whitbeck has pointed out, woman is defined as a partial man... lacking in *pnuma* or semen: the life-creating movement and force. "According to Aristotle, women, and likewise the females of other species, have less intrinsic, vital or soul heat than men, or the males of the species."[3] Thus what is lacking, or absent in woman is the movement and process that is present in the nature of man's semen. Aristotle himself says the following:

> The female in fact is female on account of an inability of a sort, viz., it *lacks* the power to concoct semen out of the final state of nourishment... [4] (my italics).

And as such, woman is defined as passive, while man

is defined as active. But more on this later.

Turning to our near contemporary, Jean-Paul Sartre, Sartre defines woman in terms of a certain kind of lack or absence. In a word, he defines woman as *hole*. He remarks:

> The obscenity of the feminine sex is that of everything which *gapes open*. It is an appeal to being as all holes are. In herself woman appeals to a strange flesh which is to transform her into a fullness of being by penetration and dissolution. Conversely, woman senses her condition as an appeal precisely because she is *in the form of a hole*. This is the true origin of Adler's complex. Beyond any doubt, her sex is a mouth and a voracious mouth which devours the penis — a fact which can easily lead to the idea of castration.[5] (Sartre's italics)

According to Sartre, then, woman is that absence of substance whose nature is to devour and eat up anything outside it. Woman, in brief, is *desire*, i.e., the wish to possess and devour what it does not by nature possess. Woman is a consuming,* reactive hole, which, like quicksand, devours, cuts off, eats, buys, etc.

Woman, says Sartre, is a gaping mouth that eats up the world, that consumes the world, because this is the only way that she, as absence, can become anything at all. Freud's little girl blames her mother for her castrated penis/clitoris. The all-consuming voracious and devouring mother has perhaps cut it off. This gaping hole, which Sartre defines as

---

* Advertisers are very well aware of this myth. That is why most advertisements are directed at woman: "the devouring and consuming sex."

woman in such terms of disgust, must of course, be filled. The absence of substance, of content, inherent in woman as hole, must be filled in with the penis — or as Sartre tells us in *Being and Nothingness*, it must be plugged up.*

> The idea of the hole is then an excavation which can be carefully molded about my flesh in such a manner that by squeezing myself into it and fitting myself tightly inside it, I shall contribute to making a fullness of being exist in the world. Thus to plug up a hole means originally to make a sacrifice of my body in order that the plenitutde of being may exist...[6]

Implicit in the above passage is the idea that woman as *hole*, as absence, is *nothingness*, and that man as plenitude is the filling flesh (penis), and the content and substance which fills the "gaping" hole of nothingness. In a word, woman is *nothingness*, man is *being*. Thus, even an ontology of woman is defined in terms of lack.

And the same may be said of Freud's ontology of sexuality. For Freud (as for most of the Western tradition), not only does woman lack and desire a penis, but furthermore, she also lacks movement or motion. That is, women are conceived as passive human beings. They are the subjects (in the strictest Hobbesian terms) of active human beings — or men.

---

* This desire to plug up a woman's vagina, is the desire of a paranoiac, to plug up woman's *flows of desire*, woman's libido, woman's sex-energy, which is, of course, always active; and to make woman a receptacle of flows instead of an active agent of flows. That is, to make her passive, and her desire reactive, and dependent upon another's — namely, man's. This is the whole idea behind the Freudian denial of the clitoris as a sexual identity for woman.

"When you say 'masculine'," says Freud, "you usually mean 'active,' and when you say 'feminine,' you usually mean 'passive'."[7] And later:

> The male sex-cell is actively mobile and searches out the female one, and the latter, the ovum, is immobile and waits passively. This behavior of the elementary sexual organisms is indeed a model for the conduct of sexual individuals during intercourse. The male pursues the female for the purpose of sexual union, seizes hold of her, and penetrates into her.[8]

As such, then, men are conceived in terms of movement or motion, and women in terms of stasis. And in relation to the last passage from *Being and Nothingness,* we can readily see how woman is equated with death, and how man is equated with life. Let us not forget that for Aristotle, life was the result of men's vital sperm.

One of the most interesting challenges made against this tradition is found in Robin Morgan's *The Anatomy of Freedom.* Morgan, like Deleuze and Guattari, appeals to the molecular level of reality, and finds there the (Bergsonian) vitalism needed to counter a passive conception of woman. Her appeal to quantum physics is an appeal to a vitalistic view of the world, and thus an appeal to *energy* — to woman, to action, to movement, etc. There is no absence of energy in black holes. As Morgan points out, black holes are composed of "energy-dense pockmarks in distant space,"[9] and their suction is understood only in relation to their creative energy, which sometimes goes by the name of "white holes."

> Physicists say: Holes are not the *absence* of par-
> ticles, but particles going faster than light.
> Flying anuses, rapid vaginas, there is no castra-
> tion.[10] (my italics)

That is correct, not even as *hole* can woman be defined
as absence or lack: woman is energy, constant movement,
flow, and her denied clitoris is just as active as the penis,
releasing flows of desire which may shatter the established
codes.

Morgan, like Deleuze and Guattari, is aware that desire is active, that desire is revolutionary, and that a philosophy of feminism must take this into account. In the end,
Deleuze and Guattari's emphasis on the importance of a micro-politics of desire is also Morgan's. "Freedom," she tells
us, "equals Energy times the square of the velocity of Transformation."[11]

2

> Polar orientations (active and initiating versus
> passive and receptive) should emerge in
> heterosexual relationships whose goal is repro-
> duction (thus, genitality is the goal for both
> sexes, and genital means vaginal for women).[12]

The above passage, by Nancy Chodorow, clearly and
succinctly describes the kind of territorialization of women's
desires made necessary by the despotism of the Oedipus

complex. Prior to reaching the Oedipal stage of "development,"* the little girl must first undergo the "realization"
that she "lacks" a penis, and secondly, the penis envy which
results from such "realization." In point of fact, the Oedipus
complex becomes the end-result of the little girl's penis
envy. The little girl first turns to the mother, but since her
mother cannot provide her with the penis, she emerges out
of her pre-Oedipal relationship with the mother, and enters
the triangulation (or better yet, strangulation) of the Oedipal
relationship with the Father. The little girl, in turn, abandons
clitoral masturbation, and replaces the clitoris as an object of
her sexual identity with the vagina, with which she now
identifies herself. And while the castration complex leads to
the dissolution of the Oedipus complex in boys, the opposite
is true for girls. It is precisely because she "lacks" a penis
that she enters the Oedipal relationship, and turns to the
Father to *provide* her with the "missing" or "castrated" penis.
She is then made to give up her feminity by transferring her
area of sexual excitation from the clitoris to the vagina. The
flows of desire released by the clitoris, and hence the *active*
and *productive* character of her sexuality is replaced by the
passive and reproductive character of her sexuality.

Women's sexuality is territorialized by psychoanalysis, and a territory — namely, the vagina — is demarcated
for her: a line is drawn between the deterritorialized flows of

---

* No, we do not believe in stages (or states of being). We believe in linear
  intensities, in flows of desires, not in spurts. And no, we do not believe
  the libido to be masculine in nature, any more than it might be exclusively feminine — the sexual character of the libido is unbounded, in
  fact, we are even hard put to speak of its character. But if one must define
  it at all, we say it is *flow*, it is process, but a process without a *telos*. There
  is no goal here, but simply, nomadic and a-topic *lines of flight*.

the clitoris and the territorialized flows of the vagina. In the end, a "No Trespassing" *sign* is placed over the former. And as our paranoiac, Sartre, describes it, the vagina becomes a receptacle, a voracious mouth, a thief, a hole that must be filled, and a territory to be colonized. And it is only when the hole is "filled," and the territory colonized, that Woman *qua* Woman is defined *for* Man.

In her novel *Blood and Guts in High School*, Kathy Acker has a drawing of a woman's legs spread apart, and above it, the following inscription: "GIRLS WILL DO ANYTHING FOR LOVE," thus pointing out the violence perpetrated on women as passive entities. This reminds us of Herzog's "Aguirre" *re*-directing all those flows, and raping all that land — the only difference is that our "Aguirre" calls himself "Oedipus."

Girls will spread their legs for love, complains Kathy Acker: but love here means *need*, a necessary condition that must be fulfilled — or more precisely, a certain kind of exchange that must take place in the phallocentric Stock Exchange of sexuality and relationships. And as Judith Van Herik remarks: "Normal femininity remains ever in the shadow of, and in *need* of love from a parental figure"[13] (my italics).

And as such, Woman as Slave remains dependent upon her Master*... a Master who can either provide or withhold affection.

––––––––––––––

* Let us keep in mind Pauline Reage's *The Story of O*, de Sade's *Justine*, and Jean de Berg's Anne — in *The Image* — whose flows are territorialized even in a public park. What is most important for us here, in terms of our last example, is Anne's triangular (or Oedipal) relationship with the other two characters, Claire and Jean. Her domination takes place within the triangle. Thus Anne, as an Oedipalized woman, becomes a symbol and an image of passitivity for all men — Anne becomes Man's

Given what we have said above, love and the phallus become one and the same for women. And the place of the Father in the Oedipal triangle, is the place of the provider, the place of the active agent, on which woman depends. Janey in *Blood and Guts*, depends completely on her father to provide her with her identity as a woman, even despite the fact that she has sex with her father regularly. "Janey," Kathy Acker tells us, "regarded her father as boyfriend, brother, sister, money, amusement, and father."[14] Thus the Father becomes a figure of authority, the Law itself, and the eternal Referent. We cannot emphasize enough the significance of this seemingly innocent word, "Provider." The father is a provider precisely because woman is defined as lack, absence, and hole. In brief, Man is what Woman is not. The Father is Capital, the Father is Money, the Father is the System, the Father is the Word, the Father is God,* the Father is Creator, the Father is the Author of Woman, and, last but not least, the Father is the World. And as a result, women must give up their clitoris as an organ of their sexuality. Of course, there is no point in resisting: hiding in the pocket of every patriarch we always find a knife. Patriarchs in primitive tribes have always used them, but of course, in all fairness, we must not forget our own "civilized" Freud: he had one also, and he used it... only the technique was different.

Man declares: there exists only One Subject, and only One Self; woman is object, and woman is Other; moreover,

---

representation of women and signified subject, and as a result Man will use both the knife and the whip.

* For an interesting treatment of the oppression of women by patriarchal religions, see Mary Daly's classic, *Beyond God the Father: Toward a Philosophy of Women's Liberation* (Beacon Press, 1973).

there exists only One flow of desire (or libido), and it, of course, is masculine. The fascism of phallocentrism demands that there only be One source of libidinal energies. Oh, yes, women's flows of desire "must" be territorialized, demarcated, and grounded, in such a way that they are only possible by coupling to the body of the One, the paranoiac or fascist. Women's flows of desire must only take place in a vertical or hier(archical) coupling: the Man on top, the Man penetrating. After all, says Freud, this is what woman wants, and this is what woman as lack *desires*. The Oedipal structure and its despotic and fascistic nature is only the articulation of such desire.

No, we do not even accept good old Oedipus as a description of human relationships — Oedipus is fascist, regardless of whether we view it as a mere description, or more forcefully, as a prescription. The internalization has already taken place through the symbolic order, and the hier(archical) frameworks have already been inscribed upon the body and psyche of women.

We want to destroy the economy of Freud's neurosis factory. Like Chaplin in *Modern Times*, we intend to use the monkey wrench we hold in our hands. We aim to liberate women's flows of desire because we've had it with fascism.

Oedipus is everywhere: Oedipus is the company Boss who harrasses women on the job, Oedipus is that "little prick" called the "psychoanalyst," Oedipus is the political despot, Oedipus is the fascist Teacher, Oedipus is God, Oedipus is the oppressive Priest, Oedipus is the brutal Cop, Oedipus is... any figure of authority. And lastly, Oedipus is the Author of *reactive desire*. Oedipus, as Deleuze and Guattari point out, introduces lack into desire, and "the imperialism of Oedipus is founded here on an absence,"[15] a fictitious absence, a symbolic absence, a mythological absence.

3

Gather round boys and girls. It is story time. Now listen: Once upon a time, there lived in ancient Greece a playwright, whose name was Sophocles. This playwright wrote a nice little play which he called *Oedipus Rex*. Two thousand years later in a distant land called Vienna, there lived a German psychiatrist whose name was Sigmund Freud. Freud read this nice little play, and suddenly he got a brilliant idea! — he was going to invent a theory of sexuality and psychology based on *Oedipus Rex* — which he did, even though it took him many, many years. He called it the "Oedipus complex." And in the end, do you know what happened? He turned everybody into a little Oedipus! And everybody has lived messed up lives ever since.

Perhaps what is most striking about the Oedipus complex is its lack of any coherent basis and its total disconnection from the Real. It is a theory based on myth and representation. It draws from the pre-rehearsed theater of antiquity, with all its established codes and cues. But what is most disturbing is that anyone at all should believe it.

"Who says that dream, tragedy, and myth are adequate to the formations of the unconscious, even if the work of transformation is taken into account?"[16] How does one go from a nice little play to a highly structuralized theory of the psyche? Where is the blueprint in *Oedipus Rex* for all those nuts and bolts so tightly fastened in the structure of the Oedipus complex? How does one jump from the world of representation to the world of psychological generative invariance? And most importantly, how is it that we have allowed our dear beloved Freud and company to crush and referentialize our desire, i.e., our active desire — or desiring-production? With the Oedipal structure, the "whole of desiring-production is crushed, subject to the requirements of representation."[17] Oedipus telling us how to live — who will believe this a hundred years from now: that there was a time when human beings were structuralized according to a nice little play? *Anti-Oedipus* already reads like science fiction.

Freud was never interested in production at all. What he wanted above all was to *re*-produce the same old scenario on the same old stage. And hence in *Oedipus* he found the kind of psychological generative invariance that would generate the same structure throughout every single aspect of life. This way there would always be Lack and the Father. "It is as if Freud had drawn back from this world of wild production and explosive desire, wanting at all costs to restore a little order there, an order made classical owing to the ancient Greek theater."[18] As Foucault remarks in *The History of Sexuality*:

> We must not forget that the discovery of the Oedipus complex was contemporaneous with the juridical organization of loss of parental authority (in France, this was formulated in the laws of 1889 and 1898). At the moment when Freud was uncovering the nature of Dora's desire and allowing it to be put into words, preparations were being made to undo those reprehensible proximities in other social sec-

tors: on the one hand, the father was elevated into an object of compulsory love, but on the other hand, if he was a loved one, he was at the same time a fallen one in the eyes of the law.[19]

And yet, the question remains: why make women the victims of this paranoia? Why referentialize and repress women's desiring-production? Perhaps the answer is quite simple; perhaps, as Guattari has said, Freud simply "despised women." But in any case, what is important for us to realize is that what we find in Freud is nothing more than representation and myth — a symbolic order, and the bit about castration, penis envy, Oedipus, and the phallus, is nothing more than a symbolic construct. For instance, what is the phallus, if not a fiction (like God), a representation, an imaginary construct, endowed with a kind of power that it does not at all possess. The phallus is not the penis but a symbolic generative invariant that reproduces itself in every aspect of life, singing the same old tune.

> In Freudian doctrine, the phallus is not a phantasy, if what is understood by that is an imaginary effect. Nor is it such an object (part internal, good, bad, etc...) insofar as this term tends to accentuate the reality involved in a relationship. It is even less the organ, penis or clitoris, which it symbolises. And it is not incidental that Freud took his reference from the simulacrum which it represented for the Ancients.[20]

The phallus is a despotic signifier or Referent before becoming an object of oppression. In effect, the phallus becomes "powerful" and hier(archical) at the moment when the mere symbolic register is transformed into actual desire.

Hence we refuse to buy Oedipus, the phallus, penis envy, castration, etc. We lack none of them, neither as men nor as women. We know very well what lies behind all these symbolic and linguistic constructs. We caught Freud throwing the anchor over-board. That is to say, territorializing and grounding desiring-production. And again, we refuse to accept Oedipus as any kind of universal Referent, descriptive or otherwise.

> Every family pattern is completely different, depending on its particular context. You don't find the same relationship to paternal authority in a shantytown in Abidjan as you find in an industrial town in Germany. Nor the same Oedipus complex, nor the same homosexuality. It seems silly to have to say anything so obvious, yet one is continually faced with disengenuous assumptions of this kind: there is *no such thing* as a *universal* structure of the mind, or of the libido!"²¹ (Guattari's italics).

Any claim to a universal structure of the mind stems from the *reactive desire* to make life mathematical, calculable, and simple, as in a story with a necessary beginning and a necessary ending. However, relationships between human beings are a lot richer than that. There are as many kinds of relationships as there are individuals. We are not even denying that there exists Oedipal relationships. But Oedipus does not come first, and it is not *the* universal Referent for all relationships.

Woman never desired the Father's penis because she never lacked it to begin with — there is nothing lacking in woman. However, what woman as a human being (not a linguistic or symbolic category) has always desired is the dissolution of the universal generative Referent that grounds her life to the phallocentric hier(archy).

> Desire is not bolstered by needs, but rather the contrary; needs are derived from desire: they are counterproducts within the real that desire produces.[22]

This is what most of the Western philosophical tradition has failed to understand, and yet what capitalism has always understood so well.

Advertisers have always known how to create myths, how to make people dependent on those myths, and lastly, how to make people feel that they lack, and of course, desire something. In effect they have always known that desire is productive; this is why they have been so successful at regulating lives. In short, advertisers have always known that "lack is a countereffect of desire," and that it is "posited, distributed, vacuolized within a real that is natural and social."[23] "Now ladies, no more rings around the collar for your husbands," and "You're not truly a woman until you use Chanel No. 5 perfume." Reactive desire then "becomes this abject fear of lacking something."[24] But what if you don't lack anything? What if a woman says to her shrink that she neither envies nor feels that she lacks a penis? What then? Oedipus collapses, and the psychoanalyst's phallus shrivels up. Heaven help us! "After all, we always thought that women were passive."

Our favorite example of rebellion against this view is found in Christine, the protagonist of Bette Gordon's film *Variety*. Christine turns the world of pornographic representation back on itself: she becomes an "intruder," observing men observing "women." Christine enters a porno shop, and through her presence there she destroys the semblance of reality in the pornographic representation of women. Oh, no, a real woman! And slowly they (the men) place the magazines back on the racks.

Christine, then, disrupts the established order, in much the same way as someone who brings a tape recorder into the psychoanalyst's office.* Christine refuses to be referentialized and grounded on representation: she does not allow desire to be produced for her, but instead produces her own desire. As Bette Gordon informs us:

> There is no representation of Christine having sex in the film. She has sex by speaking it and by voyeuristically following, [one of the patrons of the porno theater she works in]. She describes what she sees on the screen at first, but *goes on to describe what she wants to see, constructed from her own desire...* She speaks her fantasies, which silence men: they can't deal with her desire being spoken.[25] (my italics)

And they certainly can't deal with her desire being active. They want to *speak of* woman, they want to make woman an object of discursive practice, but never allow her to speak. However, Christine knows better, she knows how to shatter the codes. She knows how to destroy Oedipus...

---

*Jean-Jacques Abrahams was institutionalized for bringing a tape recorder into his psychoanalyst's office. That is, for disrupting the social order. For an interesting article by him, see *Semiotext(e)*, "Schizo-culture" issue. The article is titled, "Fuck the Talkies," 178–188.

she is active, productive, she lacks nothing — if anything, she creates the world. Her boyfriend is outraged by her fantasies, and in him Oedipus lurks. Lastly, Christine is a revolutionary, a rebel, who liberates women's flows of desire, because active desire is always revolutionary.

> Desire does not threaten a society because it is a desire to sleep with the mother, [or sleep with the father], but because it is revolutionary. And that does not at all mean that desire is something other than sexuality, but that sexuality and love do not live in the bedroom of Oedipus, they dream instead of wide-open spaces, and cause strange flows to circulate that do not let themselves be stocked within an established order. Desire does not "want" revolution, it is revolutionary in its own right, as though involuntarily, by wanting what it wants.[26]

There is no predetermined regime for desire: yes, it dreams of open spaces, and it is only free in wide-open spaces. It is only when desire is territorialized and demarcated that it becomes repressive–oppressive, as in the case of Freud and his territorialization of women's desire. The prison of women's desire is the phallocentric hier(archical) family, and her freedom is found in the actuality of rhizomatic and horizontal relationships, whether they be with other women, or men. Implicit in the freedom of women is the freedom of humanity — without it, the possibility of a non-fascist or an(archical) way of life is nil.

4

And yet, how are we to begin? How are we to transform the violence of phallocentrism into the non-violence of an(archical) relationships? For we are not concerned with replacing one hier(archical) order with another. That is to say, we are not interested in going from patriarchy to matriarchy — not even temporarily: the memory of Marx's "temporary" proletarian dictatorship remains fresh in our minds.

> The women's movement is *more* than a group governed by central authority in conflict with other such hierarchical groups. If it were only this, it would be only one more subgroup within the all-embracing patriarchal "family." What we are about is the human becoming of that half of the human race that has been excluded from humanity by sexual definition.[27] (Daly's italics)

Hence we aim to create new definitions, not so much through words, but through actions, through our an(archical) attitudes. We deny that there is any *a priori* reality to the signifier: words, and specifically certain words, are nothing more than elements within an established semiotic field, and thus we repeat, like so many other feminists, that there is no such thing as a "timeless female essence."[28] We are among the first anti-metaphysicians.

> The terms "woman" and "female body" are... free floating signifiers... which lack any constant meaning.[29]

No, we do not believe in essences, ultimate reality, Truth, or the divinity of language (we are aware of the despotic nature of the Signifier). Like Derrida, we are aware of the dictatorship of the copula: Woman is... not passivity, lack, absence, hole, etc. Woman "is" becoming, woman "is" process, woman "is" movement, etc. The copula is always despotic, its assumption is that of essences, and states, rather than flows and movement. Human beings are not simply "this" or "that," and human relationships, regardless of Oedipus, or any other fascistic structure, are not one dimensional. A life lived on one side or the other of the hier(archical) dividing line is a life lacking in richness. And as Mary Daly informs us, we can only rebel by giving up colonialization, and living on the boundary of human relations.

> Real boundary living, [she says], is a refusal of tokenism and absorption, and therefore it is genuinely dangerous.[30]

The State and other oppressive institutions are not threatened by Marxists, fanatics, etc., but by people who refuse to conform to any hier(archy) whatsoever. The most politically threatening act against the State and other established orders is the act that refuses to set up another

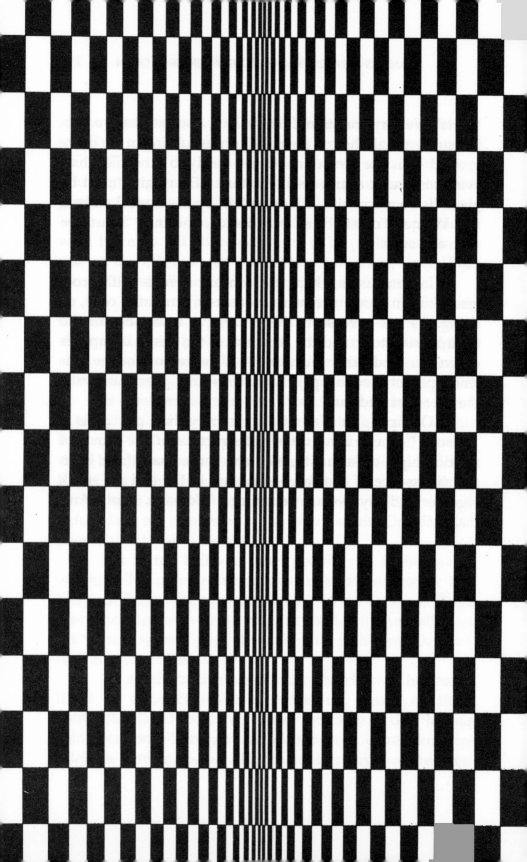

NOTES

NIETZSCHE, AN(ARCHY)
AND ANTI-PSYCHIATRY

[1] Friedrich Nietzsche, "Or Three Metamorphoses," *Thus Spoke Zarathustra*, tr. Walter Kaufmann in *The Portable Nietzsche* (N.Y.: Penguin Books, 1976), p. 139.

[2] *Ibid.*

[3] *Ibid.*

[4] Rose Pfeffer, *Nietzsche, Disciple of Dionysus* (N.J.: Bucknell University Press, 1972), p. 207.

[5] Fredrich Nietzsche, *A Nietzsche Reader*, ed. and Tr. by R. J. Hollingdale (N.Y.: Penguin Books, 1966). Aphorism #262, p. 211.

[6] Fredrich Nietzsche, "What is Noble?" *Beyond Good and Evil*, tr. Walter Kaufman (N.Y.: Vintage Books, 1966). Aphorism #391, p. 211.

[7] Gilles Deleuze, *Nietzsche and Philosophy*, tr. Hugh Tomlinson (London: The Athalone Press, 1983), pp. 60-61.

[8] Friedrich Nietzsche, *The Will to Power*, ed. Walter Kaufmann, tr. by R. J. Hollingdale and Walter Kaufmann (N.Y.: Vintage Books, 1968). Aphorism #204, p. 119.

[9] *Ibid.* Aphorism #397, p. 214.

[10] Gilles Deleuze and Felix Guattari, *Anti-Oedipus: Capitalism and Schizophrenia*, tr. Robert Hurley, Mark Seem, and Helen R. Lane (Minneapolis, Minn.: University of Minnesota Press, 1983), p. 190.

[11] Albert Camus, "Caligula," *Caligula and Three Other Plays*, tr. Stuart Gilbert (N.Y.: Vintage Books, 1958), p. 65.

[12] Friedrich Nietzsche, *The Gay Science*, tr. Walter Kaufmann (N.Y.: Vintage Books, 1974). Aphorism #109, p. 168.

[13] Friedrich Nietzsche, "On the New Idol," *Thus Spoke Zarathustra*, in *op. cit.*, p. 163.

[14] *Ibid.*, "On Self-Overcoming," p. 226.

[15] George Allen Morgan, "The Standard of Revaluation," *What Nietzsche Means* (N.Y.: Harper & Row Publishers, 1941), p. 132.

[16] Gilles Deleuze and Félix Guattari, *On the Line,* tr. John Johnston (N.Y.: Semiotext(e), 1983), p. 108.

[17] David Cooper, "On Being Born into a Family," *The Death of the Family* (N.Y.: Vintage Books, 1971), pp. 12-13.

[18] Deleuze and Guattari, *op. cit.,* p. 47.

[19] Friedrich Nietzsche, "On Child and Marriage," in *Thus Spoke Zarathustra*, in *op. cit.,* p. 182-183.

[20] Friedrich Nietzsche, "Second Essay – Section 19," *On The Genealogy of Morals*, tr. Walter Kaufmann (N.Y.: Vintage Books, 1967). Aphorism #19, pp. 88-89.

[21] Henry Miller, "The Tailor Shop," *Black Spring* (N.Y.: Grove Press, 1963), p. 111.

[22] R. D. Laing, "Rules and Metarules," *The Politics of the Family and Other Essays* (N.Y.: Vintage Books, 1972), p. 104.

[23] *Ibid.,* p. 107.

[24] David Cooper, *op. cit.,* "The End of Education," p. 73.

[25] *Ibid.,* p. 78.

[26] Deleuze and Guattari, *Anti-Oedipus*, p. 94.

[27] R. D. Laing, "The Family and the 'Family'," *The Politics of the Family and Other Essays*, p. 13.

[28] *Ibid.*, p. 13.

[29] Friedrich Nietzsche, *The Will to Power*. Aphorism #552, p. 299.

[30] Deleuze, "Politics," *On the Line*, p. 69.

AU REVOIR M. LE TEXTE, OR
THE BODY AND AN(ARCHY)

[1] Gilles Deleuze and Felix Guattari, "La Géologie de la Morale," *Mille Plateaux* (Paris: Les Editions de Minuit, 1980), pp. 53-94.

[2] Jacques Derrida, "The Theater of Cruelty," *Writing and Difference*, tr. Alan Bass (Chicago: University of Chicago Press, 1978), p. 235.

[3] Antonin Artaud, "On the Balinese Theater," *The Theater and Its Double*, tr. Mary Caroline Richards (N.Y.: Grove Press, 1958), p. 60.

[4] *Ibid.*

[5] Roland Barthes, "The Death of the Author," *Image, Music, Text*, tr. Stephen Heath (N.Y.: Hill and Wang, 1977), p. 145.

[6] *Ibid.*, p. 146.

[7] Jacques Derrida, "La parole soufflée," *Writing and Difference,* p. 187.

[8] *Ibid.,* p. 185.

[9] Antonin Artaud, "The Theater of Cruelty (Second Manifesto)," *The Theater and Its Double,* in *op. cit.,* p. 124.

[10] Roland Barthes, "The Death of the Author," *op. cit.,* p. 148.

[11] Artaud, "The Theater of Cruelty (First Manifesto)," *op. cit.,* p. 96.

[12] Artaud, "Letters on Language," *op. cit.,* p. 107.

[13] Roland Barthes, "Without Words," *Empire of Signs,* tr. Richard Howard (N.Y.: Hill and Wang, 1982). pp. 9-10.

[14] Artaud, "Oriental and Occidental Theater," *op. cit.,* p. 68.

[15] *Ibid.*

[16] Umberto Eco, "Theory of Codes," *A Theory of Semiotics* (Bloomington, Ind.: Indiana University Press, 1979), p. 64.

[17] Gilles Deleuze and Félix Guattari, *Anti-Oedipus: Capitalism and Schizophrenia,* tr. Robert Hurley, Mark Seem, and Helen R. Lane, preface by Michel Foucault (Minneapolis, Minn.: University of Minnesota Press, 1983), p. 9.

[18] Barthes. "The Written Face," *Empire of Signs,* in *op. cit.,* p. 88.

[19] *Ibid.*

[20] Antonin Artaud, "All Writing is Pigshit," *Artaud Anthology*, ed. Jack Hirschman (San Francisco, Cal: City Lights Books, 1965), p. 38.

[21] *Ibid.*

[22] *Ibid.*

[23] Marshall McLuhan, *The Gutenberg Galaxy* (Toronto, Ontario: U. of Toronto Press, 1965), p. 23.

[24] Derrida, "La parole soufflée," *op. cit.*, 175.

[25] Barthes, "From Work to Text," *Image, Music, Text*, p. 164.

[26] Roland Barthes, *The Pleasure of the Text*, tr. Richard Miller (N.Y.: Hill and Wang, 1975), p. 66.

[27] *Ibid.*, p. 42.

[28] Artaud, "No More Masterpieces," *The Theater and Its Double*, in *op. cit.*, p. 74.

[29] *Ibid.*, p. 75.

[30] *Ibid.*, p. 78.

[31] Deleuze and Guattari, *Anti-Oedipus*, p. 202.

[32] Derrida. "The Theater of Cruelty," *op. cit.*, p. 248.

[33] Artaud, "No More Masterpieces, *op. cit.*, p. 257.

[34] Jorge Amado, *Gabriela, Clove and Cinnamon,* tr. James L. Taylor and William L. Grossman (N.Y.: Alfred A. Knopf, 1962), pp. 285-298. See also the Brazilian film version with Sonia Braga.

[35] Henri Bergson, *Creative Evolution,* tr. Arthur Mitchell, foreward by Irwin Edman (N.Y.: The Modern Library, 1941), p. 141.

TOWARDS A NON-FASCIST OR AN(ARCHICAL) WAY OF LIFE

[1] Wilhelm Reich, "The Authoritarian Ideology," *The Mass Psychology of Fascism* (N.Y.: Farrar, Straus & Giroux, 1970), p. 35.

[2] Robert M. Pirsig, *Zen and the Art of Motorcycle Maintenance* (N.Y.: Bantam Books, 1975), p. 88.

[3] Gilles Deleuze and Félix Guattari, *Anti-Oedipus: Capitalism and Schizophrenia,* tr. Robert Hurley, Mark Seem and Helen R. Lane (Minneapolis, Minn.: University of Minnesota Press, 1983), p. 27.

[4] Jacques Donzelot, "An Antisociology," *Semiotext(e),* Vol. 3, No. 2 (1977): p. 36.

[5] Henry Miller, "Into the Night Life..." *Black Spring* (N.Y.: Grove Press, 1963), p. 141.

[6] Deleuze and Guattari, *Anti-Oedipus*, p. 250.

[7] Dick Hebdige, "Two Forms of Incorporation," *Subculture: The Meaning of Style* (N.Y.: Methuen, Inc., 1979), pp. 93-94.

[8] Félix Guattari, "The Role of the Signifier in the Institution," *Molecular Revolution: Psychiatry and Politics*, tr. Rosemary Sheed, Introduction by David Cooper (N.Y.: Penguin Books, 1984), pp. 75-76.

[9] Antonin Artaud, "To Have Done with the Judgment of God," a radio play (1947), *Antonin Artaud: Selected Writings*, tr. Helen Weaver, ed. with an Introduction and Notes by Susan Sontag (N.Y.: Farrar, Straus & Giroux, 1976), p. 570.

[10] Henry Miller, "Into the Night Life..." *op. cit.*, p. 141.

[11] *Anti-Oedipus*, p. 31.

[12] Deleuze and Guattari, "Balance Sheet—Program for Desiring-Machines," *Semiotext(e)*, Vol. 3, No. 2 (1977), p. 130.

[13] *Ibid.*

[14] *Ibid.*

[15] Gilles Deleuze and Félix Guattari, *On the Line*, tr. John Johnston (N.Y.: Semiotext(e), 1983), p. 22.

[16] *Ibid.* p. 15.

[17] Antonin Artaud, "Here Lies," *Artaud Anthology*, tr. F. Teri Wehn and Jack Hirschman, ed. Jack Hirschman (San Francisco, Cal.: City Lights Books, 1956), p. 238.

[18] Friedrich Nietzsche, *Selected Letters of Nietzsche*, tr. Christopher Middleton (Chicago, Ill.: University of Chicago Press, 1969), p. 347.

[19] *Anti-Oedipus*, p. 86.

[20] Eldridge Cleaver, *Soul on Ice*, with an introduction by Maxwell Geismar (N.Y.: A Delta Book, 1968), p. 5.

[21] Gilles Deleuze, "I have nothing to admit," a letter written to Michel Cressole, *Semiotext(e)*, in *op. cit.*, p. 114.

MOLECULAR REVOLUTION, ART AND AN(ARCHY)

[1] Félix Guattari, "Towards a Micro-Politics of Desire," *Molecular Revolution: Psychiatry and Politics*, tr. Rosemary Sheed, Introduction by David Cooper (N.Y.: Penguin Books, 1984), p. 90.

[2] Jacques Monod, "Invariance and Perturbations," *Chance and Necessity*, tr. Austryn Wainhouse (N.Y.: Vintage Books, 1971), p. 104.

[3] *Ibid.,* p. 100.

[4] *Ibid.,* p. 136.

[5] *Ibid.*

[6] Gilles Deleuze and Félix Guattari, *On the Line,* tr. John Johnston (N.Y.: Semiotext(e), 1983), p. 12.

[7] Jean-Françcois Lyotard, "Adrift," *Driftworks,* tr. Roger McKeon (N.Y.: Semiotext(e), 1984), p. 11.

[8] Gilles Deleuze and Félix Guattari, *Anti-Oedipus: Capitalism and Schizophrenia,* tr. Robert Hurley, Mark Seem, and Helen R. Lane (Minneapolis, Minn.: University of Minnesota Press, 1983), p. 116.

[9] Barbara Ess and Glenn Branca, editors, *Just Another Asshole,* "Some Weaknesses," Michael Gira (N.Y.: Just Another Asshole #6, 1983), p. 55.

[10] Deleuze and Guattari, *Anti-Oedipus,* p. 132.

[11] *Ibid.,* p. 135.

[12] Richard Brautigan, *Willard and His Bowling Trophies* (N.Y.: Simon & Schuster, 1975).

[13] Re/Search, "Mark Pauline," *Industrial Cultural Handbook,* issue 6/7 (San Francisco: Re/Search, 1983), pp. 23-41.

[14] William Barrett, *Time of Need, Forms of Imagination In the Twentieth Century* (Connecticut: Wesleyan University Press, 1982), p. 61.

[15] Gilles Deleuze and Félix Guattari, *Mille Plateaux*, "Devenir-intense, devenir-animal, devenir-imperceptible..." (Paris: Les Editions de Minuit, 1980), pp. 284-380.

[16] Jean-François Lyotard, "Several Silences," *Driftworks*, p. 107. Lyotard quotes Schoenberg but gives no source reference; I have quoted Lyotard quoting Schoenberg.

[17] *Ibid.*, p. 95.

[18] *Ibid.*

[19] *Ibid.*, p. 109.

[20] Re/Search, *Throbbing Gristle*, Issue 6/7, pp. 9-19.

THE FASCISTIC STRUCTURE OF REACTIVE DESIRE AND ITS RELATION TO THE DOMINATION OF WOMEN

[1] Jean Baker Miller, M.D., ed. *Psychoanalysis and Women*, "'Penis Envy' in Women," Clara Thompson (N.Y.: Penguin Books, 1973), p. 51.

[2] Plato, *The Republic*, tr. Francis McDonald Conford (N.Y.: Oxford University Press, 1941), pp. 272-273.

[3] Carol C. Gould and Marx W. Wartofsky, *Women and Philosophy: Toward a Theory of Liberation*, "Theories of Sex Difference," Caroline Whitbeck (N.Y.: G.P. Putnam's Sons, 1976), p. 55.

[4] Aristotle, *The Generation of Animals*, tr. A. L. Peck (Cambridge: Harvard University Press, 1961), p. 103.

[5] Jean-Paul Sartre, "Doing and Having," *Being and Nothingness*, tr. Hazel E. Barnes (N.Y.: Washington Square Press, 1956), p. 782.

[6] *Ibid.*, p. 781.

[7] Sigmund Freud, "Feminity," *New Introductory Lectures on Pyschoanalysis and Other Works*, tr. James Strachey, Vol. XXII (London: The Hogart Press, 1964), p. 114.

[8] *Ibid.*, p. 113.

[9] Robin Morgan, "The New Physics of Meta-politics," *The Anatomy of Freedom: Feminism, Physics, and Global Politics* (N.Y. Anchor Press/Doubleday, 1982), p. 289.

[10] *Sub/Stance* #44/45 on Gilles Deleuze, "Woman in Limbo: Deleuze and His Br(others)," Alice Jardine (Wisconsin: University of Wisconsin Press, 1985), p. 54. This is a quote from Deleuze and Gutarri's sequel to *Anti-Oedipus, Mille Plateaux*, tr. Alice Jardine. The latter text is now available from the University of Minnesota Press in a translation by Brian Massumi.

[11] *Ibid.*, p. 317.

[12] Nancy Chodorow, "Freud: Ideology and Evidence," *The Reproduction of Mothering: Psychoanalysis and the Sociology of Gender* (California: University of California Press, 1978), p. 156.

[13] Judith Van Herik, "Fulfillment and Feminity," *Freud on Femininity and Faith* (Berkeley: U. of California Press, 1982), p. 134.

[14] Kathy Acker, *Blood and Guts in High School, Plus Two* (London: Pan Books, 1984), p. 7.

[15] Gilles Deleuze and Felix Guattari, *Anti-Oedipus, Capitalism and Schizophrenia*, tr. Robert Hurley, Mark Seem, and Helen R. Lane (Minneapolis, Minn.: University of Minnesota Press, 1983), p. 58.

[16] *Ibid.*, p. 54.

[17] *Ibid.*

[18] *Ibid.*

[19] Michel Foucault, *The History of Sexuality Vol. I: An Introduction*, tr. Robert Hurley (N.Y.: Vintage Books, 1980), p. 130.

[20] Jacques Lacan (and the *École freudienne*), "The Meaning of the Phallus," *Feminine Sexuality*, ed. Juliet Mitchell and Jacqueline Rose, tr. Jacqueline Rose (N.Y.: W. W. Norton, 1985), p. 79.

21 Félix Guattari, "Molecular Revolution and Class Struggle," *Molecular Revolution: Psychiatry and Politics*, tr. Rosemary Sheed, Introduction by David Cooper (N.Y.: Penguin Books, 1984), p. 258.

22 *Anti-Oedipus*, in *op. cit.*, p. 27.

23 *Ibid.*

24 *Ibid.*

25 Carole S. Vance, ed., *Pleasure and Danger: Exploring Female Sexuality*, "Variety: The Pleasure of Looking," Bette Gordon (Boston: Routledge & Kegan Paul, 1985). This is an anthology of the papers read at the controversial Scholar and Feminist IX Conference at Barnard College in 1982.

26 *Ibid.*, p. 116.

27 Mary Daly, *Beyond God the Father: Toward a Philosophy of Women's Liberation*, (Boston: Beacon Press, 1973), p. 35.

28 Kaja Silverman, l"*Histoire d'O*: The Construction of a Female Subject," in *Pleasure and Danger*. This is a brilliant schizoanalytic reading of *The Story of O*, and specifically in terms of its critique of territorialization and the problem of representation. Excellent! p. 323.

29 *Ibid.*

[30] Mary Daly, *Beyond God the Father*, p. 55

[31] Naomi Goldenberg, "Oedipal Prisons," *Changing of the Gods* (Boston: Beacon Press, 1979), pp. 26-36.

OTHER TEXTS USED
BUT NOT CITED HEREIN

NIETZSCHE, AN(ARCHY) AND ANTI-PSYCHIATRY

Brown, Phil. *Toward a Marxist Psychology.* New York: Harper Colophon Books, 1974. Fairly good section on antipsychiatry.

Derrida, Jacques. *Writing and Difference.* Translated by Alan Bass. Chicago: University of Chicago Press, 1982. For a good account of Derrida's *"differance"* see his essay on "Differance."

Derrida, Jacques. *Positions.* Translated by Alan Bass. Chicago: Chicago University Press, 1981. In his interview with Jean-Louis Houdebine and Guy Scarpeta, Derrida differentiates between his *"differance"* and the Hegelian difference.

Goffman, Erving. *Asylums.* New York: A Doubleday Anchor Book, 1961. For a good account of total institutions, and particularly mental institutions, see this text.

Laing, R. D. *The Voice of Experience*. New York: Pantheon Books, 1982.

Sennet, Richard. *The Uses of Disorder*. New York: A Vintage Book, 1970. This is a rare book in that it treats an(archy) not as a political position, but as an attitude — as a will to live dangerously, and with chaos. It is a bit simplistic, but nevertheless a good treatment of the subject.

Szasz, Thomas S. *The Myth of Mental Illness*. New York: A Hoeber-Harper Book, 1961. A pioneering work in the area of anti-psychiatry. Of special interest for the work in this essay, see "The Rule-Following Model of Human Behavior." Not as good as Laing, but interesting nevertheless.

AU REVOIR M. LE TEXTE, OR THE BODY AND AN(ARCHY)

Baudrillard, Jean. *Simulations*. Translated by Paul Foss, Paul Patton, and Philip Beitchman. New York: Semiotext(e), Foreign Agents Series, 1983. This is an excellent book on the reproduction of signs, and the lack of distinction that exists in the postmodern world between reality and simulation, as a result of the reproduction and repetition of signs.

Elam, Keir. *The Semiotics of Theatre and Drama*. New York: Methuen, Inc., 1980. This is the best example of what happens when a structuralist takes any worthwhile idea into his or her hand. Mr. Elam asserts in his book that it was Artaud's intention to codify the gestures, when, in fact, nothing was further from Artaud's theatrical theories than this. Sorry, but Artaud was not a semiotician.

Sontag, Susan. *Under the Sign of Saturn*. New York: Farrar, Straus & Giroux, 1980. The essay which concerns us in Ms. Sontag's anthology of previously published essays is "Approaching Artaud" (pp. 13-70). This is a very good essay on Artaud, and I recommend it to anyone who is interested in approaching the latter.

Towards a Non-Fascist or An(archical) Way of Life

Butler, Samuel. *Erewhon* and *Erewhon Revisited*. N.Y.: Everyman's Library, 1959. Of special interest is the section "The Book of the Machines." Both Deleuze and Guattari are very much influenced by this section in Erewhon.

Camus, Albert. *Caligula and Three Other Plays*. Translated by Stuart Gilbert. N.Y.: Vintage Books, 1958. One of the few thinkers who has understood the violence of order has been Camus. See *Caligula* and *State of Siege* in the volume above.

Freud, Sigmund. *Three Case Histories* (The "Wolf Man," The "Rat Man," and The "Psychotic Doctor Schreber"). Introduction by Philip Reiff. N.Y.: Collier Books, 1963. The important case here is, of course, the Schreber Case, which comes up again and again in *Anti-Oedipus.*

Freud, Sigmund. *Collected Papers,* Vol. 2. London: Hogarth Press. The important essay for us here is " 'A Child Is Being Beaten': A Contribution to the Study of the Origin of Sexual Perversion."

Ionesco, Eugene. *Rhinoceros and Other Plays.* Translated by Derek Prouse. N.Y.: Grove Press, Inc., 1960. For the best example of what an(archy) means, and what constitutes an an(archist) see *Rhinoceros.*

Klein, Melanie. *Narrative of a Child Analysis: The Conduct of the Psychoanalysis of Children as Seen in the Treatment of a Ten Year Old Boy.* N.Y.: Basic Books, Inc., 1961. Melanie Klein's concept of partial objects can be found herein (pp. 18, 189, and 297). This is a very important concept in *Anti-Oedipus:* without it the coupling of desiring-machines (and what I call an(archical) desiring-machines cannot be understood.

Lacan, Jacques. *Ecrits.* Translated by Alan Sheridan. N.Y.: W. W. Norton & Company, 1977. Of special interest is the essay "On the possible treatment of psychosis," where Lacan talks about the "Name-of-the-Father" — his own linguistic Oedipalization of human beings.

Nerval, Gérard de. *Selected Writings of Gérard de Nerval.*
Translated with introduction and notes by Geoffrey
Wagner. Michigan: University of Michigan Press, 1970.
For the best example of a "schizo stroll," read "Aurelia"
(pp. 115-178).

MOLECULAR REVOLUTION, ART AND AN(ARCHY)

Ballard, J. G. *The Disaster Area.* London: Triad/Panther Books,
1967. This little book which is comprised of short stories
by Ballard is one of the most beautiful books I have ever
read. The tremendous clarity of this writer, and the
astounding affective level at which these stories are
written, makes this book a truly emotional experience.
The publisher of this book is also the publisher of *The
Unlimited Dream Company* (1979)

Ballard, J.G. *Re/Search* issue #8/9. This whole issue is devoted
to Ballard. It is comprised of interviews with Ballard,
fiction, non-fiction, and various other things. A must for
anyone interested in having a better understanding of
both his literature and Ballard himself.

Bukowski, Charles. *Notes of a Dirty Old Man.* San Francisco:
City Lights Books, 1973. This is one of my favorite pieces
by Bukowski, and it is extremely important in order to
understand what we mean here when we speak of the
non-orgasmic or linear quality of Bukowski's literature.

de Sade, The Marquis. *The Complete Justine, Philosophy in the Bedroom and Other Writings.* N.Y.: Grove Press. The important book to read here is *Philosophyy in the Bedroom,* wherein de Sade talks about the philosophy of sex. And the essays by Maurice Blanchot and Jean Paulhan which appear at the beginning of the book serve as good introductions to the philosophy of this very complex writer.

de Lautréamont, Comte. *Les Chants de Maldoror.* N.Y.: New Directions, 1946. This is a very strange book. Perhaps there has never been a book as terrifying both in its vision and its spirit as *Les Chants de Maldoror.* Not for weak stomachs.

Lewis, Wyndham. *The Complete Wild Body.* Edited by Bernard Lafourcade. Santa Barbara: Black Sparrow Press, 1982. Wyndham Lewis wrote a book in favor of Hitler before the latter came to power, and, ever since, no one has ever paid attention to the second book he wrote denouncing Hitler. It is only lately that he has received any attention at all. For an interesting account of Lewis' life, and his ideas concerning both politics and literature, see his second autobiography (*Rude Assignment*) published by Black Sparrow Press (1984). And yet the following should be made clear: none of this should be taken to mean that we agree with Lewis either on his politics or on his theories on literature — far from it, but simply that he should be taken seriously as a writer.

Miller, Henry. *Sexus: The Rosy Crucifixion.* N.Y.: Grove Press, 1965. What can one say about Miller that hasn't already been said? I mention the above text, first because it is one of my favorite texts by Miller, and secondly because Deleuze and Guattari have drawn so much from it in *Anti-Oedipus.*

Reich, Wilhelm. *The Bion Experiments.* Translated by Derek and Inge Jordan; edited by Mary Higgins and Chester M. Raphael, M.D. N.Y.: Farrar, Straus & Giroux, 1979. Reich was one of the first to have noticed the relation that exists between the molecular level and the molar and psychological level of existence. The main problem with the Bion experiments is that they were conducted according to the old Marxist concept of "dialectical materialism."

THE FASCISTIC STRUCTURE OF REACTIVE DESIRE AND ITS RELATION TO THE DOMINATION OF WOMEN

Collins, Margery L., and Pierce, Christine. "Holes and Slime: Sexism in Sartre's Psychoanalysis." From *Women and Philosophy,* Carol C. Gould and Marx W. Wartofsky, eds. An excellent critique of Sartre's psychoanalysis. Both Margery Collings and Christine Pierce have written an insightful essay on Sartre's sexism. It makes one wonder how Sartre and De Beauvoir could have gotten along.

Derrida, Jacques. *Margins of Philosophy*. Translated by Alan
   Bass. Chicago: University of Chicago Press, 1982. For an
   interesting discussion of the copula see the essay "Differance." We must also point out that deconstruction,
   taken out of its literary circle, can actually be a very
   powerful political tool of analysis. Deconstruction, even
   as it is, is a critique of the whole Western ego-centric,
   logocentric, and phallocentric tradition.

Freud, Sigmund.*Three Essays on the Theory of Sexuality*. Translated by James Strachey. N.Y.: Basic Books, 1962. The
   important section of this book for our purposes is the
   section entitled "The Differentiation Between Men and
   Women," where he goes on to discuss the masculine
   "nature" of the libido. Of course, this was not the only
   text by Freud that we used; the rest are too numerous to
   mention.

Horney, M.D., Karen. *Feminine Psychology*. Edited with an
   introduction by Harold Kelman, M.D. N.Y.: W. W.
   Norton, 1967. This is an interesting book on feminine
   psychoanalysis, but there is very little in it that one
   would say is "earth shattering."

Mitchell, Juliet. *Psychoanalysis and Feminism*. N.Y.: Vintage
   Books, 1974. This is the most reactionary book on
   feminism and psychoanalysis that we have ever come
   across. In fact, a great deal of this essay has been written
   to prove that one cannot call oneself a "feminist" and
   then in the same breath say that one is also a "psychoanalyst." It is like saying that one is against anti-Semi-
   tism, and that one is also a Nazi.

Additional Semiotext(e) / Autonomedia Titles

FATAL STRATEGIES
JEAN BAUDRILLARD

A major work by the controversial author of *Simulations, In the Shadow of the Silent Majorities, Forget Foucault, The Ecstasy of Communication, The Critique of the Political Economy of the Sign, The Mirror of Production,* and *America,* offering "fatal alternatives" to the failure of radical responses to postmodernity. Topics range from modes of political representation and strategies of refusal to aesthetic theory and commodification, situationist theory, seduction, gambling and obesity.
Now Available — $12 postpaid

AESTHETICS OF DISAPPEARANCE
PAUL VIRILIO

From infantile narcolepsy to the illusion of movement in speed, the author of *Pure War , Speed and Politics, The Lost Dimension,* and other works examines the "aesthetic" of disappearance: in film,
in politics, in war, in the philosophy of subjectivity, and elsewhere.
Now Available — $10 postpaid

COLUMBUS & OTHER CANNIBALS
THE WÉTIKO DISEASE & THE WHITE MAN
JACK D. FORBES

A noted American Indian scholar and activist examines the heritage of indigenous American cultures since the coming of Europeans in the 15th century, with a particular focus on the "wétiko disease," the White Man's fascination with the exploitation and control of nature and his fellow man.
Spring, 1991 — $12 postpaid

"GONE TO CROATAN"
ORIGINS OF AMERICAN DROPOUT CULTURE
JAMES KOEHNLINE & PETER LAMBORN WILSON, EDITORS

Studies of lost American history and the cultures of disappearance, including "tri-racial isolate" communities, the bucaneers, "white Indians," black Islamic movements, the Maroons of the Great Dismal Swamp, scandalous eugenics theories, rural "hippie" communes, and many other aspects of American autonomous cultures.
A *festschrift* in honor of historian Hugo Leaming Bey of the Moorish Science Temple.
Spring, 1991 — $12 postpaid

TROTSKYISM AND MAOISM
THEORY AND PRACTICE IN FRANCE & THE U.S.A.
A. BELDEN FIELDS

An important examination of the critical heritage
of Trotsky and Mao in two Western national
contexts, focusing on the multitudinous parties
and sects and their positions on national and
international issues, racism, sexism, party / worker
positions, gay rights, and students movements.
Charts of organizational histories.
Now Available — $12 postpaid

MODEL CHILDREN
MY SOVIET SUMMERS AT ARTEK
PAUL THOREZ

The son of long-time French Communist Party
chief Maurice Thorez recounts his post-war
childhood experiences at Artek, the prestigious
Crimean summer camp for children of the Soviet
elite, where he saw aspects of Russian political
culture rarely revealed to the West.
Photos and Maps.
Now Available — $12 postpaid

Additional Semiotext(e) / Autonomedia Titles

MARX BEYOND MARX
LESSONS ON THE GRÜNDRISSE
ANTONIO NEGRI

A key figure in the Italian "Autonomia"
Movement reads Marx's *Gründrisse,* developing
the critical and controversial theoretical apparatus
that informs the "refusal of work" strategy and
many other elements so crucial to this "heretical"
tendency in Marxist theory. A provocative
challenge to both capitalist and / or socialist
apologists for waged slavery, whether by private
business or the State.
Now Available — $12 postpaid

RETHINKING MARXISM
STRUGGLES IN MARXIST THEORY
STEPHEN RESNICK & RICHARD WOLFF, EDITORS

Contributions from 25 leading Marxist economists
and political scientists assessing the current state
of world politics, including Bettelheim, Mandel,
Amin, Miliband, Wallerstein, O'Connor, Payer,
Gunder Frank, Bowles and Gintis, Genovese,
dedicated to the work of Paul Sweezy, Harry
Magdoff and the *Monthly Review* school.
Now Available — $14 postpaid

Additional Semiotext(e) / Autonomedia Titles

ABOUT FACE
RACE IN POSTMODERN AMERICA
TIMOTHY MALIQALIM SIMONE
Joining the theoretical insights of postmodernist
critics and philosophers like Lyotard, Baudrillard,
Derrida and others with work in Afrocentric
ethnology, psychology, and anthropology, Simone
examines the ethics and politics of race and racial
experience in contemporary America.
Now Available — $12 postpaid

SCANDAL
ESSAYS IN ISLAMIC HERESY
Peter Lamborn Wilson
A search for the "poetic facts" of heresy in
Islamic history, ranging from "sacred pederasty"
in Persian sufism and forbidden imagery in
Islamic art, to the inner teachings of the Assassins,
the heretical influences on "Shiite terrorism,"
and the mystical uses of wine, opium and
hashish, by the author of *Drunken Universe*
and *Angels: An Illustrated Study*.
Now Available — $11 postpaid